Readings in Catholic Social Teaching

Readings in Catholic Social Teaching

Selected Documents of
the Universal Church, 1891–2011

Compiled by
John T. Richardson, CM

WIPF & STOCK · Eugene, Oregon

READINGS IN CATHOLIC SOCIAL TEACHING
Documents of the Universal Church, 1891–2011

Copyright © 2015 John T. Richardson. All rights reserved. Except for brief quotations in critical publications or reviews, no part of this book may be reproduced in any manner without prior written permission from the publisher. Write: Permissions, Wipf and Stock Publishers, 199 W. 8th Ave., Suite 3, Eugene, OR 97401.

Wipf & Stock
An Imprint of Wipf and Stock Publishers
199 W. 8th Ave., Suite 3
Eugene, OR 97401

www.wipfandstock.com

ISBN 13: 978-1-62564-555-5

Contents

Preface | vii
Chronological List of Documents | ix
Alphabetical List of Documents | xiii

1 Human Dignity
  A. Foundations | 1
  B. Rights | 7
  C. Duties | 16
  D. Human Dignity and International Common Good | 19

2 Social Structures and Functions
  A. Marriage and the Family | 25
  B. Education | 32
  C. Population | 36
  D. Community and Particular Characteristics | 41

3 Development
  A. Christian Vision | 50
  B. Urgency and Fullness of Development | 53
  C. Development, Wealthy and Developing Nations | 58

D. Development, Constant and Changing, Failures and Successes | 60

  E. Theological Dimensions | 65

4 Economic Justice

  A. Growing Awareness of God-Given, Rational Ideas of Justice in the Economy | 68

  B. Public, Private Ownership | 75

  C. Economy, International Cooperation | 79

  D. Environment, Ecology, Consumerism | 83

5 Labor

  A. Work Basic to Life, Dignity | 86

  B. Labor and Society | 91

  C. Organization of Labor | 92

  D. Duties and Rights of Labor | 94

  E. Some Labor Problems | 96

6 Political Community

  A. Political Community and Public Authority | 100

  B. Citizen Participation | 104

  C. Political Community and the Church | 105

  D. Peace | 107

  E. International Community | 112

  F. Liberation Theology | 114

7 Church and Society

  A. Universality of Mission | 118

  B. Church and Social Responsibility | 121

  C. Some Characteristics of Church Teaching | 122

Bibliography | 127
Subject Index | 131
Source Index | 134

Preface

THESE READINGS FORM A short summary of the universal Catholic social teaching from Pope Leo XIII in 1891 to the pontificate of Pope Benedict XVI in 2011.

Each reading is an excerpt from a notable Catholic document, with the source of each reading given at the end of the quotation. These are mostly papal encyclicals and documents of the Second Vatican Council. Hence, the readings are official or authentic in their source and universal in their application. Some are inspirational as well. They serve multiple purposes: as an invitation to delve deeper into the vast and growing treasury of writings on social justice, a starting point for thoughtful discussion for better understanding the contemporary value of these documents, an opportunity for prayerful reflection, or a college theology textbook. The topical, rather than chronological, ordering of the readings brings all of these teachings developed by different ecclesiastics over many generations together into seven major themes of social teaching, each of which forms the subject of a chapter.

The readings invite a personal acceptance of the values of the documents, deeper than an intellectual understanding. This reflects Cardinal Newman's idea that "The heart speaks to the heart" (*Cor ad cor loquitur*).

Preface

The first chapter is foundational, for it describes the source of this teaching in understanding the dignity of the human person. The philosophical bases for this moral teaching are strong, as can be seen, for example, in the teaching of the Stoics and the Enlightenment. Far stronger, however, is the Christian theological base. In becoming a human person, God significantly raised the dignity of all people by sharing their human nature.

This book presents only the universal Catholic social teaching issued under direct papal or conciliar authority. Bishops around the world, either individually for their own dioceses or as members of a national conference of bishops, regularly publish their own social teachings, which are in conformity with universal teachings but are directed more or less to social issues of their own diocese or country.

Over the ages, theologians have also contributed to the development of Catholic social teaching. Some of their ideas on social issues have been so broadly accepted that they have become a source for developing official social documents.

A critical examination of these teachings reveals their developmental character and sometimes even radical changes in thinking. This development can be credited to the continuous inspiration of the Holy Spirit, new theological thinking, and continuous changes in the culture of societies around the world that require fresh theological directions—for instance, recent globalization. These developments not only expand or alter Catholic social teaching, but in certain instances, also radically change it. For example, Vatican Council II document *Dignitatis Humanae* explains religious freedom in a way directly contrary to the explanations of pre-Vatican II popes.

This book is titled *Catholic Social Teaching* to emphasize an openness to fresh inspiration and thinking, in contrast to the title *Catholic Social Doctrine* regularly used in Vatican documents to emphasize the magisterial authority underlying such official documents and the consistency of these documents over many generations. These readings are called *teaching* to stress further their developmental character and place them in the category of other theological topics that are advancing notably, thanks to continued inspiration and research.

Chronological List of Documents

RN *Rerum Novarum*: The Condition of Labor
(Leo XIII, 1891)

QA Quadragismo Anno: After Forty Years (Pius XI, 1931)

MM Mater et Magistra: Christianity and Social Progress
(John XXIII, 1961)

PT Pacem in Terris: Peace on Earth (John XXIII, 1963)

LG Lumen Gentium: Dogmatic Constitution on the Church
(Second Vatican Council, 1965)

GS Gaudem et Spes: Pastoral Constitution on the Church in
the Modern World (Second Vatican Council, 1965)

DH Dignitatis Humanae: Declaration of Religious Freedom
(Second Vatican Council, 1965)

NA Nostra Aetate: Declaration on the Relations of the Church to
Non-Christian Religions (Second Vatican Council, 1965)

GE Gravissimum Educationis: Declaration on Christian Education (Second Vatican Council, 1965)

Chronological List of Documents

PUN Address of Paul VI to the General Assembly of the United Nations (October 4, 1965)

PP Populorum Progressio: On the Development of Peoples (Paul VI, 1967)

OA Octogesimo Adveniens: A Call to Action on the Eightieth Anniversary of the Rerum Novarum (Paul VI, 1971)

JW Justice in the World (Synod of Bishops, 1971)

EN Evangelii Nuntiandi: Evangelization in the Modern World (Paul VI, 1975)

RH Redemptor Hominis: Redeemer of Humankind (John Paul II, 1979)

DM Dives in Misericordia: Rich in Mercy (John Paul II, 1980)

LE Laborem Exercens: On Human Work (John Paul II, 1981)

SRS Sollicitudo Rei Socialis: On Social Concern (John Paul II, 1987)

EC Ecological Crisis: A Common Responsibility (John Paul II, 1990)

CA Centesimus Annus: On the Hundredth Anniversary of Rerum Novarum (John Paul II, 1991)

VS Veritatis Splendor (John Paul II, 1993)

GA Gratissimam Sane (John Paul II, 1994)

CSDC Compendium of the Social Doctrine of the Church (Pontifical Council for Justice and Peace, 2004)

DC Deus Caritas Est: Christian Love (Benedict XVI, 2005)

CV Caritas in Veritate: Integral Human Development in Charity and Truth (Benedict XVI, 2009)

Chronological List of Documents

TR Towards Reforming the International Financial and Monetary System in the Context of Global Public Authority (Pontifical Council for Justice and Peace, 2011)

Alphabetical List of Documents

CA   Centesimus Annus: On the Hundredth Anniversary of Rerum Novarum (John Paul II, 1991)

CSDC Compendium of the Social Doctrine of the Church (Pontifical Council for Justice and Peace, 2004)

CV   Caritas in Veritate: Integral Human Development in Charity and Truth (Benedict XVI, 2009)

DC   Deus Caritas Est: Christian Love (Benedict XVI, 2005)

DH   Dignitatis Humanae: Declaration of Religious Freedom (Second Vatican Council, 1965)

DM   Dives in Misericordia: Rich in Mercy (John Paul II, 1980)

EC   Ecological Crisis: A Common Responsibility (John Paul II, 1990)

EN   Evangelii Nuntiandi: Evangelization in the Modern World (Paul VI, 1975)

GA   Gratissimam Sane (John Paul II, 1994)

Alphabetical List of Documents

GE Gravissimum Educationis: Declaration on Christian Education (Second Vatican Council, 1965)

GS Gaudem et Spes: Pastoral Constitution on the Church in the Modern World (Second Vatican Council, 1965)

JW Justice in the World (Synod of Bishops, 1971)

LE Laborem Exercens: On Human Work (John Paul II, 1981)

LG Lumen Gentium: Dogmatic Constitution on the Church (Second Vatican Council, 1965)

MM Mater et Magistra: Christianity and Social Progress (John XXIII, 1961)

NA Nostra Aetate: Declaration on the Relations of the Church to Non-Christian Religions (Second Vatican Council, 1965)

OA Octogesimo Adveniens: A Call to Action on the Eightieth Anniversary of the Rerum Novarum (Paul VI, 1971)

PP Populorum Progressio: On the Development of Peoples (Paul VI, 1967)

PT Pacem in Terris: Peace on Earth (John XXIII, 1963)

PUN Address of Paul VI to the General Assembly of the United Nations (October 4, 1965)

QA Quadragismo Anno: After Forty Years (Pius XI, 1931)

RH Redemptor Hominis: Redeemer of Humankind (John Paul II, 1979)

RN Rerum Novarum: The Condition of Labor (Leo XIII, 1891)

SRS Sollicitudo Rei Socialis: On Social Concern (John Paul II, 1987)

Alphabetical List of Documents

TR Towards Reforming the International Financial and Monetary System in the Context of Global Public Authority: (Pontifical Council for Justice and Peace, 2011)

VS Veritatis Splendor (John Paul II, 1993)

1

Human Dignity

A. Foundations

1. The Crown of Creation

ACCORDING TO THE ALMOST unanimous opinion of all, believers and unbelievers alike, all things on earth should be related to man as their center and crown. (*Gaudium et Spes*, GS 12)

For the Sacred Scripture teaches that man was created "to the image of God," is capable of knowing and loving his Creator, and was appointed by him as master of all earthly creatures that he might subdue them and use them to God's glory. "What is man that thou art mindful of him or the son of man that thou visitest him? Thou has made him a little less than the angels, thou has crowned him with glory and honor, thou has subjected all things under his feet" (Ps 8:56). (GS 12)

Prizing highly the marvelous biblical message, the Church's social doctrine stops to dwell above all on the principal and indispensable dimension of the human person. Thus it is able to grasp the most significant facets of the mystery and dignity of human beings. In the past there has been no lack of various reductionist concepts of the human person, many of which are still dramatically present on the stage of modern history. These are ideological in character or are simply the result of widespread forms of custom or thought concerning mankind, human life, and human destiny. (*Veritatis Splendor*, VS 64)

The common denominator among these is the attempt to make the image of man unclear by emphasizing only one of his characteristics at the expense of all the others. (VS 64)

2. Christ and Human Dignity

Christ is the perfect man who has restored in the children of Adam the likeness of God. By his Incarnation he, the Son of God, has, in a certain way, united himself with each man. He worked with human hands; he thought with a human mind, acted with a human will, and with a human heart he loved. (*Redemptor Hominis*, RH 8)

Charity is the heart of the church's social doctrine. Every responsibility and every commitment spelled out by that doctrine is derived from charity which, according to the teaching of Jesus, is the synthesis of the entire law. It gives real substance to the personal relationship with God and with neighbor; it is the principle not only of micro-relationships with friends, with family members, or within small groups, but also of macro-relationships, social, economic, and political ones. (*Caritate in Veritate*, CV 2)

3. The Human Person: A Mystery and Center of a Struggle between Good and Evil

But what is man? About himself he has expressed, and continues to express, many divergent and even contradictory opinions. In these he often exalts himself as the measure of all things or debases himself to the point of despair. The result is doubt and anxiety. (GS 12)

Although he was made by God in a state of holiness, from the very dawn of history man abused his liberty at the urging of Personified Evil. Man set himself against God and sought to find fulfillment apart from God. Although he knew God, he did not glorify him as God, but his senseless mind was darkened and he served the creature rather than the Creator. (GS 13)

Therefore man is split within himself. As a result, all of human life, whether individual or collective, shows itself to be a dramatic struggle between good and evil, between light and darkness. Indeed, man finds that by himself he is incapable of battling the assaults of evil successfully, so that everyone feels as though he is bound by chains. (GS 13)

But the Lord himself came to free and strengthen man, renewing him inwardly and casting out that prince of this world who held him in the bondage of sin. For sin has diminished man, blocking his path to fulfillment. (GS 13)

The call to grandeur and the depths of misery are both part of human experience. They find their ultimate and simultaneous explanation in the light of God's revelation. (GS 13)

4. Man: One Body and Soul

Though made of body and soul, man is one. Through his bodily composition, he gathers to himself the elements of the material world. Thus they reach their crown through him, and through him, raise their voice in free praise of the Creator. (GS 14)

For this reason man is not allowed to despise his bodily life. Rather, he is obliged to regard his body as good and honorable since God has created it and will raise it up on the last day. Nevertheless, wounded by sin, man experiences rebellious stirrings in his body. But the very dignity of man postulates that man glorify God in his body and forbid it to serve the evil inclinations of his heart. (GS 14)

Now, man is not wrong when he regards himself as superior to bodily concerns and as more than a speck of nature or a nameless constituent of the city of man. For by his interior qualities he outstrips the whole sum of mere things. He finds reinforcement in his profound insight whenever he enters into his own heart. God, who probes the heart, awaits him there. There he discerns his proper destiny beneath the eyes of God. Thus, when man recognizes within himself a spiritual and immortal soul, he is not being mocked by a deceptive fantasy springing from mere physical or social influences. On the contrary, he is getting to the depth of the very truth of the matter. (GS 14)

5. Intellect and Search for Penetrating Truths

Man judges rightly that by his intellect he surpasses the material universe, for he shares in the light of the divine mind. By relentlessly applying his talents through the ages, he has indeed made progress in the practical sciences, technology, and the liberal arts. In our time he has won superlative victories, especially in his probing the material world and in subjecting it to himself. (GS 15)

Still he has always searched for more penetrating truths, and he finds them. For his intelligence is not confined to observable data alone. It can with genuine certitude attain to reality itself as knowable. Though in consequence of sin that certitude is partly obscured and weakened. (GS 15)

The intellectual nature of the human person is perfected by wisdom and needs to be. For wisdom gently attracts the mind of man to a quest and a love for what is true and good. Steeped in wisdom, man passes through visible realities to those which are unseen. (GS 15)

Our era needs such wisdom more than bygone ages if the discoveries made by man are to be further humanized. For the future of the world stands in peril unless wise men are forthcoming. It should also be pointed out that many nations, poorer in economic goods are quite rich in wisdom and can offer noteworthy advantages to others. It is, finally, through the gift of the Holy Spirit that man comes by faith to the contemplation and appreciation of the divine plan. (GS 15)

6. Dignity of Human Conscience

In the depths of his conscience, man detects a law which he does not impose on himself, but which holds him to obedience. Always summoning him to love good and avoid evil, the voice of conscience can, when necessary, speak to his heart more specifically: do this, shun that. For man has in his heart a law written by God. To obey it is the very dignity of man according to which he will be judged. (GS 16)

Conscience is the most secret core and sanctuary of a man. There he is alone with God whose voice echoes in his depths. In a wonderful manner, conscience reveals that law which is fulfilled by love of God and neighbor. In fidelity to conscience, Christians are joined by the rest of men in search for truth and for the genuine solution to the numerous problems which arise in the life of individuals and from social relationships. Hence the more that a correct conscience holds sway, the more persons and groups turn aside from blind choice and strive to be guided by objective norms of morality. (GS 16)

Conscience frequently errs from invincible ignorance without losing its dignity. The same cannot be said of a man who cares little for truth and goodness or of a conscience which by degrees grows practically sightless as a result of habitual sin. (GS 16)

7. Excellence of Liberty

Only in freedom can man direct himself toward goodness. Our contemporaries make much of this freedom and pursue it eagerly, and rightly so, to be sure. Often, however, they foster it perversely as a license for doing whatever pleases them, even if it is evil. (GS 17)

For its part, authentic freedom is an exceptional sign of the divine image within man. For God has willed that man be left in the hand of his own counsel so that he can seek his Creator spontaneously and come freely to utter and blissful perfection through loyalty to Him. Hence man's dignity demands that he act according to a knowing and free choice. Such a choice is personally motivated and prompted from within. It does not result from blind internal impulse nor from mere external pressure. (GS 17)

Man achieves such dignity when emancipating himself from all captivity to passion; he pursues his goal in a spontaneous choice of what is good and procures for himself, through effective and skilled action, apt means to that end. Since man's freedom has been damaged by sin, only by the help of God's grace can he bring such a relationship with God into full flower. Before the judgment seat of God each man must render an account of his own life, whether he has done good or evil. (GS 17)

We thus come to the very heart of the Gospel truth about *freedom*. The person realizes himself by the exercise of freedom in truth. Freedom cannot be understood as a license to do *absolutely anything;* it means a gift of self. Even more: it means an *interior discipline of the gift*. The idea of gift contains not only the free initiative of the subject but also the aspect of duty. (*Gratissimam Sane*, GA 14)

In the exercise of their freedom, men and women perform normally good acts that are constructive for society when they are obedient to truth, that is, when they do not presume to be the creators and absolute masters of truth or ethical norms (*Catechism of the Catholic Church*). Freedom, in fact, does not have its absolute and unconditional origin in itself but in the life within which it is situated and which offers, at one and the same time, both a limitation and a possibility. Human freedom belongs to us as creatures; it is a freedom which is given as a gift, one to be received like a seed and to be cultivated responsibly. When the contrary is the case, freedom dies, destroying man and society. (VS 86)

8. Man Is Social by Nature

But God did not create man as a solitary being. From the beginning "male and female he created them" (Gen 1:27). Their companionship produces the primary form of inter personal communion. For by his innermost nature man is a social being, and unless he relates himself to others he can neither live nor develop his potential. (GS 12)

9. Death and Man's Destiny in God

It is in the face of death that the riddle of human existence becomes most acute. God called man and still calls him so that with his entire being he might be joined to him in an endless sharing of a divine life beyond all corruption. Christ won this victory when he rose to life, since by his death he freed man from death. Hence to every thoughtful man a solidly established faith provides the answer to his anxiety about what the future holds for him. At the same time, faith gives him the power to be united in Christ with his loved ones who have already been snatched away by death. Faith arouses the hope that they have found the true life with God. (GS 18)

B. Rights

Fundamental human dignity finds its fulfillment in the acknowledgment and exercise of rights in man's life with God and society. The realization of the individual person's destiny and good order in society would be impossible without these rights. In his 1963 encyclical *Pacem in Terris* (PT), Pope John XXIII briefly presents the Church's position on this topic. Other encyclicals and documents of Vatican II have confirmed and expanded his teaching.

1. The Source of Rights in the Nature of Man

How strongly does the turmoil of individual men and peoples contrast with the perfect order of the universe! It is as if the relationships which bind them together could be controlled only by force. (*Pacem in Terris*, PT 4)

But the Creator of the world has imprinted in man's heart an order which his conscience reveals to him and enjoins him to obey. (PT 5).

And how could it be otherwise? For whatever God has made shows forth his infinite wisdom, and it is manifested more clearly in the things which have greater perfection. (PT 5)

But fickleness of opinion often produces this error: that many think that the relationships between men and states can be governed by the same laws as the forces and irrational elements of the universe, whereas the laws governing them are of a quite different kind and are to be sought elsewhere, namely, where the Father of all things wrote them, that is, in the nature of man. (PT 6)

By these laws men are most admirably taught, first of all, how they should conduct their mutual dealings among themselves; next, how the relationships between the citizens and the public authorities of each state should be regulated; then, how the states should deal with one another; finally, how on the one hand individual men and states, and on the other hand the community of all peoples should act toward each other; the establishment of such a world community of peoples being urgently demanded today by the requirements of the universal common good. (PT 7)

2. Rights, Order in Human Society, and Revealed Truth

Any human society, if it is to be well-ordered and productive, must lay down as a foundation this principle, namely, that every human being is a person, that is, his nature is endowed with intelligence and free will. By virtue of this, he has rights and duties of his own, flowing directly and simultaneously from his very nature. These rights are therefore universal, inviolable, and inalienable. (PT 9)

If we look upon the dignity of the human person in the light of divinely revealed truth, we cannot help but esteem it far more highly. For men are redeemed by the blood of Jesus Christ. They are by grace the children and friends of God and heirs of eternal glory. (PT 10)

3. Basic Rights, Defined Separately but Interdependent and Mutually Supportive

a. Life

Beginning our discussion of the rights of man, we see that every man has the right to life, to bodily integrity, and to the means which are necessary and suitable for the proper development of life. These means are primarily food, clothing, shelter, rest, medical care, and finally, necessary social services. Therefore, a human being also has the right to security in cases of sickness, inability to work, widowhood, old age, unemployment, or in any other case in which he is deprived of the means of subsistence through no fault of his own. (PT 11)

b. Moral and Cultural Values

By the natural law, every human being has the right to respect for his person, to his good reputation, to freedom in searching for truth and—within limits laid down by the moral order and the common good—expressing and communicating his opinions, and in the pursuit of art. He has, finally, to be informed truthfully about public events. (PT 12)

The natural law also gives man the right to share in the benefits of culture and therefore the right to a basic education or to a technical or professional training in keeping with the stage of educational development in the country to which he belongs. Every effort should be made to insure that persons be enabled, on the basis of merit, to go on to higher studies, so that, as far as possible, they may occupy posts or take on responsibilities in human society in accordance with their natural gifts and the skills they have acquired. (PT 13)

c. Worship God According to Conscience

Every human being has the right to honor God according to the dictates of an upright conscience and the right to profess his religion privately and publicly. For, as Lactantius so clearly taught: "We were created for the purpose of showing to the God who bore us the due submission we owe him, of recognizing him alone, and of serving him. We are obliged and bound by this duty to God; from this, religion itself receives its name." (PT 14, confirmed and expanded in the declaration *Dignitatis Humanae*, DH of Vat. II)

And on this point our predecessor of immortal memory, Leo XIII, declared: "This genuine, this honorable freedom of the sons of God, which most nobly protects the dignity of the human person, is greater than any violence or injustice; it has always been sought by the Church, and always most dear to Her. This was the freedom which the Apostles claimed with intrepid constancy, which the Apologists defended with their writings, and which the Martyrs in such numbers consecrated with their blood." (PT 14)

The demand for freedom in human society chiefly regards the quest for the values proper to the human spirit. It regards, in the first place, the free exercise of religion in society. (DH 1)

This Vatican Synod takes careful note of these desires in the minds of men. It proposes to declare them to be greatly in accord with truth and justice. To this end, it searches into the sacred tradition and doctrine of the Church—the treasury out of which the Church continually brings forth new things which are in harmony with the things that are old. (DH 1)

First, this sacred Synod professes its belief that God himself has made known to mankind the way in which men are to serve him, and thus be saved in Christ and come to blessedness. We believe that this one true religion subsists in the one catholic and apostolic church, to which the Lord Jesus committed the duty of spreading it abroad among all men. Thus he spoke to the apostles: "Go, therefore, and make disciples of all nations, baptizing them in the name of the Father, and of the Son, and of the Holy Spirit, teaching them to observe all that I have commanded you" (Matt

28:19–20). On their part, all men are bound to seek the truth, especially in what concerns God and his Church, and to embrace the truth they come to know, and to hold fast to it. (DH 1)

This sacred Synod likewise professes its belief that it is upon the human conscience that these obligations fall and exert their binding force. The truth cannot impose itself except by virtue of its own truth, as it makes its entrance into the mind at once quietly and with power. Religious freedom, in turn, which men demand as necessary to fulfill their duty to worship God, has to do with immunity from coercion in civil society. Therefore, it leaves untouched traditional Catholic doctrine on the moral duty of men and societies toward the true religion and toward the one church of Christ. (DH 1)

Over and above all this, in taking up the matter of religious freedom this sacred Synod intends to develop the doctrine of recent Popes on the inviolable right of the human person and on the constitutional order of society. (DH 1)

The Synod further declares that the right to religious freedom has its foundation in the very dignity of the human person, as this dignity is known through the revealed word of God and by reason itself. This right of the human person to religious freedom is to be recognized in the constitutional law whereby society is governed. Thus it is to become a civil right. (DH 2)

In accordance with their dignity as human persons—that is, being endowed with reason and free will and therefore privileged to bear personal responsibility—all men should be at once impelled by nature and also bound by a moral obligation to seek the truth, especially religious truth. They are also bound to adhere to the truth, once it is known, and to order their whole lives in accord with the demands of truth. (DH 2)

However, men cannot discharge these obligations in a manner in keeping with their own nature unless they enjoy immunity from external coercion as well as psychological freedom. Therefore, the right to religious freedom has its foundation not in the subjective disposition of the person, but in its very nature. In consequence, the right to this immunity continues to exist even in those who do not live up to their obligation of seeking the truth and adhering to it. Nor is the exercise of this right to be impeded, provided that the just requirements of public order are observed. (DH 2)

Truth, however, is to be sought after in a manner proper to the dignity of the human person and his social nature. The inquiry is to be free, carried on with the aid of teaching or instruction, communication, and dialogue. In the course of these, men explain to one another the truth they have discovered, or think they have discovered, in order thus to assist one another in the quest for truth. Moreover, as truth is discovered, it is by a personal assent that men are to adhere to it. (DH 3)

On his part, man perceives and acknowledges the imperatives of the divine law through the mediation of conscience. In all of his activities, man is bound to follow his conscience faithfully, in order that he may come to God, for whom he was created. It follows that he is not to be forced to act in a manner contrary to his conscience. Nor, on the other hand, is he to be restrained from acting in accordance with his conscience, especially in matters religious. (DH 3)

There is further consideration. The religious acts whereby men, in private or in public and out of a sense of personal conviction, direct their lives to God transcend by their very nature the order of terrestrial and temporal affairs. Government, therefore, ought indeed to take account of the religious life of the people and show it favor, since the function of government is to make provision for the common welfare. However, it would clearly transgress the limits set to its power were it to presume to direct or inhibit acts that are religious. (DH 3)

Provided the just requirements of public order are observed, religious bodies rightfully claim freedom in order that they may govern themselves according to their own norms, honor the Supreme Being in public worship, assist their members in the practice of the religious life, strengthen them by instruction, and promote institutions in which they may join together for the purpose of ordering their own lives in accordance with their religious principles. (DH 4)

Since the family is a society in its own original right, it has the right freely to live its own domestic religious life under the guidance of parents. Parents, moreover, have the right to determine, in accordance with their own religious beliefs, the kind of religious education that their children are to receive. (DH 5)

The right to religious freedom is exercised in human society; hence its exercise is subject to certain regulatory norms. In the use of all freedoms, the moral principle of personal and social responsibility is to be observed. In the exercise of their rights, individual men and social groups are bound by the moral law to have respect both for the rights of others and their own duties for the common welfare of all. Men are to deal with their fellows in justice and civility. (DH 7)

d. Freely Choose One's State of Life

Human beings have the right to choose freely the state of life which they prefer. They therefore have the right to set up a family, with equal rights and duties for man and woman, and also the right to follow a vocation to the priesthood or the religious life. (PT 15)

The family, grounded on marriage freely contracted, monogamous and indissoluble, must be considered the first and essential cell of human society. To it must be given, therefore, every consideration of an economic, social, cultural, and moral nature which will strengthen its stability and facilitate the fulfillment of its specific mission. (PT 16)

Parents, however, have a prior right in the support and education of their children. (PT 17)

e. Economic

When we turn to the economic sphere, it is clear that human beings have the natural right to free initiative in the economic field and the right to work. (PT 18)

Indissolubly linked with those rights is the right to working conditions in which physical health is not endangered, morals are safeguarded, and young people's normal development is not impaired. Women have the right to working conditions in accordance with their requirements and their duties as wives and mothers. (PT 19)

From the dignity of the human person there also arises the right to carry on economic activities according to the degree of responsibility of which one is capable. Furthermore—and this must be specially emphasized—there is the worker's right to a wage determined according to criteria of justice. This means, therefore, one sufficient, in proportion to the available resources, to give the worker and his family a standard of living in keeping with human dignity. In this regard, our predecessor Pius XII said: "To the personal duty of work imposed by nature, there corresponds and follows the natural right of each individual to make of his work the means to provide for his own life and the lives of his children; so profoundly has nature ordained the preservation of man" (Radio Message, June 1, 1941). (PT 20)

The right to private property, even of productive goods, also derives from the nature of man. This right, as we have elsewhere declared, " . . . is a suitable means for safeguarding the dignity of the human person and for the exercise of responsibility in all fields; it strengthens and gives serenity to family life, thereby increasing the peace and prosperity of the state." (PT 21)

However, it is opportune to point out that there is a social duty inherent in the right of private property. (PT 22)

f. Assembly and Association

From the fact that human beings are by nature social, there arises the right of assembly and association. They have also the right to give the societies of which they are members the form they consider most suitable for the aim they have in view and to act within such societies on their own initiative and responsibility in order to achieve their desired objective. (PT 23)

Human Dignity

We ourselves strongly cautioned in the encyclical *Mater et Magistra* that, for the achievement of ends which individual human beings cannot attain except by association, it is necessary and indispensable to set up a great variety of intermediate groups and bodies in order to guarantee the dignity of human persons and safeguard a sufficient sphere of freedom and responsibility. (PT 24)

g. Emigration and Immigration

Every human being must have the right to freedom of movement and of residence within the confines of his own country, and, when there is just reason for it, the right to emigrate to other countries and take up residence there. The fact that one is a citizen of a particular state does not detract in any way from his membership in the human family or from his citizenship in the world community and his common tie with all men. (PT 25)

h. Political Participation and Protection

The dignity of the human person involves, moreover, the right to take an active part in public affairs and to contribute one's part in the common good of the citizens. For as our predecessor of happy memory Pius XII points out: "The human individual, from being an object and, as it were, a merely passive element in the social order, is, in fact, must be, and continue to be, its subject, its foundation and its end" (Radio Message, Dec. 24, 1944). (PT 26)

The human person is also entitled to a juridical protection of his rights, a protection that should be efficacious, impartial, and in conformity with true norms of justice. (PT 27)

As our predecessor Pius XII warns: "That perpetual privilege proper to man, by which every individual has a claim to the protection of his rights, and by which there is assigned to each a definite and particular sphere of rights, immune from all arbitrary attacks, is the logical consequence of the order of justice willed by God." (PT 27)

C. Duties

Pope John XXIII in *Pacem in Terris* teaches that the understanding and exercise of human rights is incomplete without a corresponding understanding and fulfillment of human duties.

1. The Inseparable Connection of Rights and Duties.

The natural rights with which we have been dealing are, however, inseparably connected, in the very person who is their subject, with just as many respective duties. And rights as well as duties find their source, their sustenance, and their inviolability in the natural law which grants or enjoins them. (PT 28)

For example, the right of every man to life is correlative with the duty to preserve it; his right to a decent standard of living, with the duty of living it becomingly, and his right to investigate the truth freely, with the duty of pursuing it ever more completely and profoundly. (PT 29)

2. Reciprocity of Rights and Duties between Persons

Once this is admitted, it is also clear that in human society to one man's natural right there corresponds a duty in other persons: the duty, namely, of acknowledging and respecting the right in question. For every fundamental human right draws its indestructible moral force from the natural law, which, in granting it, imposes a corresponding obligation. Those, therefore, who claim their own rights, yet altogether forget or neglect to carry out their respective duties, are people who build with one hand and destroy with the other. (PT 30)

Since men are social by nature, they are meant to live with others and to work for one another's welfare. Hence, a well-ordered human society requires that men recognize and observe their mutual rights and duties. It also demands that each contribute generously to the establishment of a civil order in which rights and duties are progressively more sincerely and effectively acknowledged and fulfilled. (PT 31)

It is not enough, for example, to acknowledge and respect every man's right to the means of subsistence. One must also strive to insure that he actually has enough in the way of food and nourishment. (PT 32)

The society of men must not only be organized but must also provide them with abundant resources. This, certainly, requires that they recognize and fulfill their mutual rights and duties. It also requires that they all collaborate in many enterprises that modern civilization either allows or encourages or even demands. (PT 33)

3. An Attitude of Responsibility

The dignity of the human person also requires that every man enjoy the right to act freely and responsibly. For this reason, in social relations especially, man should exercise his rights, fulfill his obligations, and, in countless forms of collaboration with others, act chiefly on his own responsibility and initiative. This is to be done in such a way that each one acts on his own decision, of set purpose and from consciousness of his obligation, without being moved by force or pressure brought to bear on him externally. (PT 34)

For any human society that is established on the sole basis of force must be regarded as simply inhuman, inasmuch as the freedom of its members is repressed, when in fact they should be provided with appropriate incentives and means for developing and perfecting themselves. (PT 34)

4. Duties in Social Life: Truth, Justice, Charity, Freedom

A political society is to be considered well ordered, beneficial, and in keeping with human dignity if it is grounded on truth. As the Apostle Paul exhorts us: "Wherefore, put away lying and speak truth each with his neighbor, because we are members of one another" (Eph 4:25). This indeed will be the outcome when reciprocal rights and duties are sincerely recognized. (PT 35)

Furthermore, human society will be such as we have just described it, if the citizens, guided by justice, apply themselves seriously to respecting the rights of others and discharging their own duties; if they are moved by such fervor of charity as to make their own the needs of others and share with others their own goods; if, finally, they everywhere work for a progressively closer fellowship in the world of spiritual values. Moreover, human society is realized in freedom, that is to say, by ways and means in keeping with the dignity of its citizens who accept the responsibility of their actions precisely because they are by nature rational beings. (PT 35)

Human society, venerable brothers and beloved children, ought to be regarded above all as a spiritual reality; one in which men communicate knowledge to each other in the light of truth; in which they can enjoy their rights and fulfill their duties and are inspired to strive for goods of the spirit. Society should enable men to share in and enjoy every legitimate expression of beauty. It should encourage them constantly to pass on to the others all that is best in themselves, while they strive to make their own the spiritual achievements of others. These are the values which continually give life and basic orientation to cultural expressions, economic and social institutions, political movements and forms, laws, and all other structures by which society is outwardly established and constantly developed. (PT 36)

The order which prevails in society is by nature moral. Grounded as it is in truth, it must function according to the norms of justice; it should be inspired and perfected by mutual love; finally, it should be brought to an ever more refined and human balance in all freedom. (PT 37)

Now an order of this kind, whose principles are universal, absolute, and unchangeable, has its ultimate source in the one true God, who is personal and transcends human nature. Inasmuch as God is the first truth and the highest good, he alone is that deepest source from which human society can draw its vitality, if that society is to be well ordered, beneficial, and in keeping with human dignity. (PT 38)

As St. Thomas Aquinas says, "Human reason is the norm of the human will, according to which its goodness is measured, because reason derives from the eternal law which is the divine reason itself. It is evident then that the goodness of the human reason depends much more on the eternal law than on human reason" (*Summa Theol.*, Ia–IIae q.19, a.4). (PT 38)

D. Human Dignity and International Common Good

Globalization has incorporated the dignity of the human person into the world order. Every day marks an increase in the influence international decisions and events have on the individual person and societies in all nations of the world. Especially since the time of Pope John XXIII, the pontiffs have developed the teaching of the church on human dignity and the world order.

1. Rights and Duties of Political Communities

Our predecessors have constantly maintained, and we join them in reasserting, that political communities are reciprocally subjects of rights and duties. This means that their relationships also must be harmonized in truth, in justice, in an active solidarity, and in freedom. The same moral law which governs relations between individual human beings serves also to regulate the relations of political communities with each other. (PT 80)

Furthermore, authority is a necessary requirement of the moral order in human society. It may not, therefore, be used against that order; the very instant such an attempt were made, it would cease to be authority, as the Lord has warned us: "Hear, therefore, kings and understand; learn, you magistrates of the earth's expanse! Hearken, you who rule the multitude and lord it over throngs of peoples! Because authority was given you by the

Lord and sovereignty by the Most High, who shall probe your works and scrutinize your counsels" (Wis 6:1–4)! (PT 83)

Lastly, it is to be borne in mind that also in the regulating of relations between political communities, authority is to be exercised for the achievement of the common good, which constitutes the reason for it existence. (PT 34)

2. The Universal Common Good

The unity of the human family has always existed because its members are human beings all equal by virtue of their natural dignity. Hence there will always exist the objective need to promote in sufficient measure the universal common good, that is, the common good of the entire human family. (PT 132)

In times past, one could be justified in feeling that the public authorities of the different political communities might be in a position to provide for the universal common good, either through normal diplomatic channels or top-level meetings, or by making use of juridical instruments such as conventions and treaties or other means suggested by the natural law, or by the law of nations or by international law. (PT 133)

As a result of the far-reaching changes which have taken place in relations of the human family, on the one hand the universal common good gives rise to problems which are complex, very grave, and extremely urgent, especially as regards security and world peace. On the other hand, the public authorities of the individual political communities—placed as they are on a footing of equality one with the other—no matter how much they multiply their meetings or sharpen their wits in efforts to draw up new juridical instruments, are no longer able to face the task of finding an adequate solution to the problems mentioned above. And this is not due to a lack of good will or of a spirit of enterprise but because of a structural defect which hinders them. (PT 134)

It can be said, therefore, that at this historical moment the present system of organization and the way its principle of authority operates on a world basis no longer correspond to the objective requirements of the universal common good. (PT 135)

Like the common good of individual political communities, so too the universal common good cannot be determined except by having regard to the human person. Therefore, the public authority of the world community, too, must have as its fundamental objective the recognition, respect, safeguarding, and promotion of the human person. This can be done by direct action when required, or by creating on a world scale an environment in which the public authorities of the individual political communities can more easily carry out their specific functions. (PT 139)

3. Address of Pope Paul VI to the General Assembly of the United Nations, 4 October, 1965 (PUN)

To speak of humanity and generosity is to invoke another basic principle of the United Nations Organization, and also its noblest aim: for it is not just to avert conflicts between nations that you labor here; you also seek to make it possible for them to work for one another. You are not satisfied merely with furthering coexistence between countries; you do something far better, something that deserves our praise and our support: you promote the brotherhood of peoples. In this way a system of solidarity is set up, and its lofty civilized aims win the orderly and unanimous support of the family of peoples for the common good and for the good of each individual. This aspect of the organization of the United Nations is the most beautiful; it is its most truly human visage; it is the ideal of mankind in its pilgrimage through time; it is the world's greatest hope; it is, we presume to say, the reflection of the loving and transcendent design of God for the progress of the human family on earth—a reflection in which we see the message of the Gospel which is heavenly become earthly. Indeed, it seems to us that we hear the echo of the voice of our predecessors, and particularly that of Pope John XXIII, whose message of *Pacem in Terris* was so honorably and significantly received among you. (PUN 25)

You proclaim here the fundamental rights and duties of man, his dignity, his freedom—and above all his religious freedom. We feel that you thus interpret the highest sphere of human wisdom and, we might add, its sacred character. For you deal here above all with human life; and the life of man is sacred; no one may dare offend it. Respect for life, even with regard to the great problem of birth, must find here in your Assembly its highest affirmation and its most reasoned defense. You must strive to multiple bread so that it suffices for the tables of mankind, and not rather favor an artificial control of birth, which would be irrational, in order to diminish the number of guests at the banquet of life. (PUN 26)

It does not suffice, however, to feed the hungry; it is necessary also to assure to each man a life conformed to his dignity. This too you strive to perform. We may consider this the fulfillment before our very eyes, and by your efforts, of that prophetical announcement so applicable to your institution: "They will melt down their swords into ploughshares, their spears into pruning forks" (Isa 2:4). Are you not using the prodigious energies of the earth and the magnificent inventions of science, no longer as instruments of death but as tools of life for humanity's new era? (PUN 27)

4. The View of the Church on the United Nations Universal Declaration of Human Rights

An act of the highest importance enacted by the United Nations was the Universal Declaration of Human Rights, approved in the General Assembly on December 10, 1948. In the preamble of that declaration, the recognition and respect of those rights and respective liberties is proclaimed as an ideal to be pursued by all peoples and all countries. (PT 143)

Some objections and reservations, we observed, were raised regarding certain points in the declaration, and rightly so. There is no doubt, however, that the document represents an important step on the path toward the juridico-political organization of the world community. For in it, in most solemn form, the dignity of the human person is acknowledged in all men. And as a consequence there is proclaimed, as a fundamental right, the right of free movement in the search for truth and in the attainment of moral good and of justice, and also a right to a dignified life, while other rights connected with those mentioned are likewise proclaimed. (PT 144)

It is our earnest prayer that the United Nations—in its structure and in its means—may become ever more equal to the magnitude and nobility of its tasks. May the day come as quickly as possible when every human being will find therein an effective safeguard for the rights which derive directly from his dignity as a person, and which are therefore universal, inviolable, and inalienable rights. This is all the more to be hoped for since all human beings, as they take an ever more active part in the public life of their own communities, are showing an increasing interest in the affairs of all peoples, and are becoming more consciously aware that they are living members of a world community. (PT 145)

5. Growing Universal Concern for Human Dignity and Personal Rights

The first positive note is the full awareness among large numbers of men and women of their own dignity and that of every human being. This awareness is expressed, for example, in the more lively concern that human rights should be respected and in the more vigorous rejection of their violation. One sign of this is the number of recently established private associations, some worldwide in membership, almost all of them devoted to monitoring with great care and commendable objectivity what is happening internationally in this sensitive field. *(Sollicitudo Rei Socialis,* SRS 26)

At this level one must acknowledge the influence exercised by the Declaration of Human Rights, promulgated some forty years ago by the United Nations Organization. Its very existence and gradual acceptance by the international community are signs of a growing awareness. The same is to be said, still in the field of human rights, of other juridical instruments issued by the United Nations Organization or other international organizations. (SRS 26)

The awareness under discussion applies not only to individuals but also to nations and peoples, which, as entities having a specific cultural identity, are particularly sensitive to the preservation, free exercise, and promotion of their precious heritage. (SRS 26)

At the same time, in a world divided and beset with every type of conflict, the conviction is growing of a radical interdependence and consequently of the need for a solidarity which will take up interdependence and transfer it to the moral plane. Today, perhaps more than in the past, people are realizing that they are linked together by a common destiny, which is to be constructed together if catastrophe for all is to be avoided. From the depth of anguish, fear, and escapist phenomena like drugs, typical of the contemporary world, the idea is slowly emerging that the good to which we are all called and the happiness to which we all aspire cannot be obtained without an effort and commitment on the part of all, nobody excluded, and the consequent renouncing of personal selfishness. (SRS 26)

2

Social Structures and Functions

A. Marriage and the Family

1. The Foundation of Human and Christian Society

THE WELL-BEING OF THE individual person and of human and Christian society is intimately linked with the healthy condition of that community produced by marriage and the family. Hence Christians and all men who hold this community in high esteem sincerely rejoice in the various ways by which men today find help in fostering this community of love and perfecting its life, and by which spouses and parents are assisted in their lofty calling. Those who rejoice in such aids look for additional benefits from them and labor to bring them about. (GS 47)

Yet the excellence of this institution is not everywhere reflected with equal brilliance. For polygamy, the plague of divorce, so-called free love, and other disfigurements have an obscuring effect. In addition, married love is too often profaned by excessive self-love, the worship of pleasure, and illicit practices against human generation. Moreover, serious disturbances are caused in families by modern economic conditions, by influences at once social and psychological, and by the demands of civil society. Finally, in certain parts of the world problems resulting from population growth are generating concern. (GS 47)

All these situations have produced anxious consciences. Yet, the power and strength of the situation of marriage can also be seen in the fact that time and again, despite the difficulties produced, the profound changes in modern society reveal the true character of this institution in one way or another. (GS 47)

2. Sanctity of Marriage and Family

The intimate partnership of married life and love has been established by the Creator and qualified by His laws. It is rooted in the conjugal covenant of irrevocable personal consent. Hence, by that human act whereby spouses mutually bestow and accept each other, a relationship arises which by divine will and in the eyes of society too is a lasting one. For the good of the spouses and their offspring as well as of society, the existence of this sacred bond no longer depends of human decisions alone. (GS 48)

For God Himself is the author of matrimony, endowed as it is with various benefits and purposes. All of these have a decisive bearing on the continuation of the human race, on the personal development and the eternal destiny of the individual members of the family, and on the dignity, stability, peace, and prosperity of the family itself and human society as a whole. By their very nature, the institution of matrimony itself and conjugal love are ordained for the procreation and education of children, and find in them their ultimate crown. (GS 48)

Thus a man and a women, who by their marriage covenant of conjugal love "are no longer two, but one flesh" (Matt 19:6) render mutual help and service to each other through an intimate union of their persons and of their actions. Through this union they experience the meaning of their oneness and attain to it with growing perfection day by day. As a mutual gift of two persons, this intimate union, as well as the good of the children, imposes total fidelity on the spouses and argues for an unbreakable oneness between them. (GS 48)

Christ the Lord abundantly blessed this many-faceted love, welling up as it does from the fountain of divine love and structured as it is on the model of His union with the Church. For as God of old made Himself present to his people through a covenant of love and fidelity, so now the savior of men and the Spouse of the Church come into the life of married Christians through the sacrament of matrimony. He abides with them thereafter so that, just as he loved the church and handed himself over on her behalf, the spouses may love each other with perpetual fidelity through mutual self-bestowal. (GS 48)

Authentic married love is caught up into divine love and is governed and enriched by Christ's redeeming power and the saving activity of the Church. Thus can love lead the spouses to God with powerful effect and can aid and strengthen them in the sublime office of being a father or mother. (GS 48)

For this reason, Christian spouses have a special sacrament by which they are fortified and receive a kind of consecration in the duties and dignity of their state. By virtue of this sacrament, as spouses fulfill their conjugal and family obligations, they are penetrated with the spirit of Christ, which suffuses their whole lives with faith, hope, and charity. Thus they increasingly advance their own perfection, as well as their mutual sanctification, and hence contribute jointly to the glory of God. (GS 48)

As a result, with their parents leading their way by example and family prayer, children and indeed everyone gathered around the family hearth will find a readier path to human maturity, salvation, and holiness. Graced with the dignity and office of fatherhood and motherhood, parents will energetically acquit themselves of a duty which devolves primarily on them, namely education, and especially religious education. (GS 48)

As living members of the family, children contribute in their own way to making their parents holy. For they will respond to the kindness of their parents with sentiments of gratitude, with love and trust. They will stand by them as children should when hardships overtake their parents and old age brings its loneliness. Widowhood, accepted bravely as a continuation of the marriage vocation, will be esteemed by all. Families will share their spiritual riches generously with other families too. Thus the Christian family, which springs from marriage as a reflection of the loving covenant uniting Christ with the Church, and as a participation in that covenant, will manifest to all men the Savior's living presence in the world and the genuine nature of the Church. This the family will do by the mutual love of the spouses, by their generous fruitfulness, their solidarity and faithfulness, and by the loving way in which all members of the family work together. (GS 48)

The social subjectivity of the family, both as a single unit and associated in a group, is expressed as well in the demonstrations of solidarity and sharing not only among families themselves but also in the various forms of participation in social and political life. This is what happens when the reality of the family is founded on love: being born in love and growing in love, solidarity belongs to the family as a constitutive and structural element. (VS 50)

This is a solidarity that can take on features of service and attention to those who live in poverty and need, to orphans, the handicapped, the sick, the elderly, to those who are in mourning, to those with doubts, to those who live in loneliness or who have been abandoned. It is a solidarity that opens itself to acceptance, to guardianship, to adoption; it is able to bring every situation of distress to the attention of institutions so that, according to their specific competence, they can intervene. (VS 50)

Far from being only objects of political action, families can and must become active subjects, working to see that the law and institutions of the state not only do not offend but support and positively defend the rights and duties of the family. (VS 50)

Welcoming human life in the united aspect of its physical and spiritual dimensions, families contribute to the communion of generations and in this way provide essential and irreplaceable support for the development of society. For this reason the family has a right to assistance by society in the bearing and rearing of children. Those married couples who have a large family have a right to adequate aid and should not be subject to discrimination. (VS 34)

3. Conjugal Love

The biblical Word of God several times urges the betrothed and the married to nourish and develop their wedlock by pure conjugal love and undivided affection. Many men of our own age also highly regard true love between husband and wife as it manifests itself in a variety of ways depending on the worthy customs of various peoples and times. (GS 49)

This love is an eminently human one since it is directed from one to another through an affection of the will. It involves the good of the whole person. Therefore it can enrich the expressions of body and mind with a unique dignity, ennobling these expressions as special ingredients and signs of the friendship distinctive of marriage. (GS 50)

Such love, merging the human with the divine, leads the spouses to a free and mutual giving of themselves, a gift proving itself by gentle affection and by deed. Such love pervades the whole of their lives. Indeed, by generous activity it grows better and it grows greater. Therefore it far excels mere erotic inclination, which, selfishly pursued, soon enough fades wretchedly away. (GS 49)

This love is uniquely expressed and perfected through the marital act. The actions within marriage by which the couple are united intimately and chastely are noble and worthy ones. Expressed in a manner which is truly human, these actions signify and promote that self-giving by which spouses enrich each other with a joyful and thankful will. (GS 49)

Authentic conjugal love will be more highly prized, and wholesome public opinion created regarding it, if Christian couples give outstanding witness to faithfulness and harmony in that same love, and to their concern for educating their children; also, if they do their part in bringing about the needed cultural, psychological, and social renewal on behalf of marriage and the family. (GS 49)

Especially in the heart of their own families, young children should be aptly and seasonably instructed about the dignity, duty, and expression of married love. Trained thus in the cultivation of chastity, they will be able at a suitable age to enter a marriage of their own after an honorable courtship. (GS 49)

It is essential to engage in a battle, at the national and international levels, against the violations of the dignity of boys and girls caused by sexual exploitation by those caught up in pedophilia and every kind of violence directed against these most defenseless of human creatures. These are criminal acts that must be effectively fought with adequate preventive and penal measures by the determined action of the different authorities involved. (VS 61)

4. Fruitfulness of Marriage, Deciding the Number of Children, Purposes of Marriage

Marriage and conjugal love are by their very nature ordained toward the begetting and educating of children. Children are really the supreme gift of marriage and contribute very substantially to the welfare of their parents. The God Himself who said, "It is not good for man to be alone" (Gen 2:18) and "who made man from the beginning male and female" (Matt 19:4), wished to share with man a certain special participation in His own creative work. Thus he blessed male and female, saying, "Increase and multiply" (Gen 2:28). (GS 50)

Parents should regard as their proper mission the task of transmitting human life and educating those to whom it has been transmitted. They should realize that they are thereby cooperators with the love of God the Creator, and are, so to speak, the interpreters of that love. Thus they will fulfill their task with human and Christian responsibility. With docile reverence toward God, they will come to the right decision by common counsel and effort. (GS 50)

They will thoughtfully take into account both their own welfare and that of their children, those already born and those which may be foreseen. For this accounting they will reckon with both the material and spiritual conditions of the times as well as their

Social Structures and Functions

state in life. Finally, they will consult the interests of the family group, of temporary society, and of the Church herself. (GS 50)

The parents themselves should ultimately make this judgment in the sight of God. But in their manner of acting, spouses should be aware that they cannot proceed arbitrarily. They must be governed according to a conscience dutifully conformed to the divine law itself. (GS 50)

Thus, trusting in Divine Providence and refining the spirit of sacrifice, married Christians glorify the Creator and strive toward fulfillment in Christ when, with a generous human and Christian sense of responsibility, they acquit themselves of the duty to procreate. Among the couples who fulfill their God-given task in this way, those merit special mention who with wise and common deliberation, and with a gallant heart, undertake to bring up suitably a relatively large family. (GS 50)

Marriage to be sure is not instituted solely for procreation. Rather, its very nature as an unbreakable compact between persons and the welfare of the children both demand that the mutual love of spouses, too, be embodied in a rightfully ordered manner, that it grow and ripen. Therefore, marriage persists as a whole manner and communion of life, and maintains its value and indissolubility, even when offspring are lacking—despite, rather often, the very intense desire of the couple. (GS 50)

The first and fundamental structure for "human ecology" is the family, in which man receives his first formative ideas about truth and goodness and learns what it means to love and to be loved, and thus what it actually means to be a person. Here we mean the family founded on marriage in which the mutual gift of self by husband and wife creates an environment in which children can be born and develop their potentialities, become aware of their dignity and prepare to face their unique and individual destiny. But it often happens that people are discouraged from creating the proper conditions for human reproduction and are led to consider themselves and their lives as a series of sensations to be experienced rather than as a work to be accomplished. The result is a lack of freedom, which causes a person to reject a commitment to enter into a stable relationship with another person and to bring children into the world, or which leads people to consider children as one of the "many things" which an individual can have or not have, according to taste, and which compete with other possibilities. (*Centesimus Annus*, CA 39)

B. Education

Although education has its roots and primary functions in the family, learning and formation constitute an integral part of the livelong development of the person and community. The Second Vatican Council formulated a declaration on Christian Education, *Gravissimum Educationis* (GE). Additional documents highlight different sources of education and different topics instructive of the comprehensive role of education.

1. Education Ennobling and Pervasive of Christian Living

Since every man of whatever race, condition, and age is endowed with the dignity of a person, he has an inalienable right to an education corresponding to his proper destiny and suited to his native talents, his sex, his cultural background, and his ancestral heritage. At the same time, this education should pave the way to brotherly association with other peoples, so that genuine union and peace on earth may be promoted. For a true education aims at the formation of the human person with respect to his ultimate goal and simultaneously with respect to the good of those societies of which, as a man, he is a member and in whose responsibilities, as an adult, he will share. (*Gravissimum Educationis*, GE 1)

As a consequence, with the help of advances in psychology and in the art and science of teaching, children and young people should be assisted in the harmonious development of their physical, moral, and intellectual endowments. Surmounting hardships with a gallant and steady heart, they should be helped to acquire gradually a more mature sense of responsibility toward ennobling their own lives through constant effort and toward pursuing authentic freedom. As they advance in years, they should be given positive and prudent sexual education. Moreover, they should be trained to take their part in social life so that by proper instruction in necessary and useful skills they can become actively involved in various community organizations, be ready for dialogue with others, and be willing to act energetically on behalf of the common good. (GE 1)

Among all of the agencies of education, the school has a special importance. By virtue of its very purpose, while it cultivates the intellect with unremitting attention, the school ripens the capacity for right judgment, provides an introduction into the cultural heritage won by past generations, promotes a sense of values, and readies for professional life. By creating friendly contacts between students of different temperament and background, the school fosters among them a willingness to understand one another. Moreover, the school sets up a kind of center whose operation and progress deserve to engage the joint participation of families, teachers, various kinds of cultural, civic, and religious groups, civil society, and the entire human community. (GE 5)

The Church is keenly aware of her very grave obligation to give zealous attention to the moral and religious education of all her children. To those large numbers of them who are being trained in schools which are not Catholic, she needs to be present with her special affection and helpfulness. This she does through the living witness of those who teach and direct such students, through the apostolic activity of their schoolmates, but most of all through the services of priests and laymen who transmit to them the doctrine of salvation in a way suited to their age and circumstances and who afford them spiritual assistance through programs which are appropriate under the prevailing conditions of time and setting. (GE 7)

The Church's involvement in the field of education is demonstrated especially by the Catholic school. No less than other schools does the Catholic school pursue cultural goals and the natural development of youth. But it has several distinctive purposes. It aims to create for the school community an atmosphere enlivened by the Gospel spirit of freedom and charity. It aims to help the adolescent in such a way that the development of his own personality will be matched by the growth of that new creation which we became by baptism. It strives to relate all human culture eventually to the news of salvation, so that the light of faith will illumine the knowledge which students gradually gain of the world, of life, and of mankind. (GE 8)

At the diocesan, national, and international level, the spirit of cooperation grows daily more urgent and effective. Since this same spirit is most necessary in educational work, every effort should be made to see that suitable coordination is fostered between various Catholic schools, and that between these schools and others that kind of collaboration develops which the well-being of the whole human family demands. (GE 12)

2. Challenges of Education in a Developing World

It is our opinion that the inconsistency between religious faith, in those who believe, and their activities in the temporal sphere, results—in great part—from the lack of a solid Christian education. Indeed, it happens in many quarters and too often that there is no proportion between scientific training and religious education. The former continues and is extended until it reaches higher degrees, while the latter remains at the elementary level. (PT 153)

It is indispensable, therefore, that in the training of youth, education should be complete and without interruption; that is to say, religious values should be cultivated in the minds of the young and their moral conscience refined in a manner to keep pace with the continuous and ever more abundant assimilation of scientific and technological knowledge. And it is indispensable, too, that they be instructed regarding the proper way to carry out their actual tasks. (PT 153)

We deem it opportune to point out how difficult it is to understand clearly the relation between the objective requirements of justice and concrete situations, that is, to perceive the degrees and forms in which doctrinal principles and directives ought to be applied to current human affairs. (PT 154)

Educational method must be such as to teach men to live their lives in its entire reality and in accord with evangelical principles of personal and social morality which are expressed in the vital Christian witness of one's life. (*Justice in the World*, JW 49)

But education demands a renewal of heart, a renewal based on the recognition of sin in its individual and social manifestations. It will also inculcate a truly and entirely human way of life in justice, love and simplicity. It will likewise awaken a critical sense, which will lead us to reflect on the society in which we live and on its values; it will make men ready to renounce these values when they cease to promote justice for all men. In the developing countries, the principal aim of this education for justice consists in an attempt to awaken consciences to a knowledge of the concrete situation and in a call to secure a total improvement; by these means the transformation of the world has already begun. (JW 51)

Since this education makes men decidedly more human, it will help them to be no longer the object of manipulation by communications media or political forces. It will instead enable them to take in hand their own destinies and bring about communities which are truly human. (JW 52)

Accordingly, this education is deservedly called a continuing education, for it concerns every person and every age. It is also a practical education: it comes through action, participation, and vital contact with the reality of injustice. (JW 53)

Gentlemen, you have performed and you continue to perform a great work: the education of mankind in the ways of peace. The U.N. is the great school where that education is imparted, and we are today in the assembly hall of that school. Everyone who takes his place here becomes a pupil and also a teacher in the art of building peace. When you leave this hall, the world looks upon you as the architects and constructors of peace. (PUN 21)

C. Population

More recently, the question often is raised how economic organization and the means of subsistence can be balanced with population increase, whether in the world as a whole or within the needy nations. (*Mater et Magistra*, MM 185)

As regards the world as a whole, some, consequent to statistical reasoning, observe that within a matter of decades mankind will become very numerous, whereas economic growth will proceed much more slowly. From this, some conclude that unless procreation is kept with limits, there subsequently will develop an even greater imbalance between the number of inhabitants and the necessities of life. (MM 186)

It is clearly evident from statistical records of less developed countries, that, because recent advances in public health and in medicine are there widely diffused, the citizens have a longer life expectancy consequent to lowered rates of infant mortality. The birth rate, where it has been traditionally high, tends to remain at such levels, at least for the immediate future. Thus the birth rate in a given year exceeds the death rate. Meanwhile the productive systems in such countries do not expand as rapidly as the number of inhabitants. Hence, in poorer countries of this sort, lest a serious crisis occur, some are of the opinion that the conception or birth of humans should be avoided or curbed by every possible means. (MM 187)

Now to tell the truth, the interrelationships on a global scale between the number of births and available resources are such that we can infer grave difficulties in this matter do not arise at present, nor will in the immediate future. The arguments advanced in this connection are so inconclusive and controversial that nothing certain can be drawn from them. (MM 188)

Besides, God in His goodness and wisdom, has, on the one hand, provided nature with almost inexhaustible capacity; and on the other hand, has endowed man with such ingenuity that, by using suitable means, he can apply nature's resources to the needs and requirements of existence. Accordingly, that the question

Social Structures and Functions

posed may be clearly resolved, a course of action is not indeed to be followed whereby, contrary to the moral law laid down by God, procreative function also is violated. Rather, man should, by the use of his skills and science of every kind, acquire an intimate knowledge of the forces of nature and control them ever more extensively. Moreover, the advances hitherto made in science and technology give almost limitless promise for the future in this matter. (MM 189)

When it comes to questions of this kind, we are not unaware that in certain locales and also in poorer countries, it is often argued that in such an economic and social order difficulties arise because citizens, each year more numerous, are unable to acquire sufficient food or sustenance where they live, and people do not show amicable cooperation to the extent they should. (MM 190)

But whatever be the situation, we clearly affirm these problems should be posed and resolved in such a way that man does not have recourse to methods and means contrary to his dignity, which are proposed by persons who think of man and his life solely in material terms. (MM 191)

We judge that this question can be resolved only if economic and social advances preserve and augment the genuine welfare of individual citizens and of human society as a whole. Indeed, in a matter of this kind, first place must be accorded everything that pertains to the dignity of man as such, or to the life of individual men, than which nothing can be more precious. Moreover, in this matter, international cooperation is necessary, so that, conformably with the welfare of all, information, capital, and men themselves may move about among the peoples in orderly fashion. (MM 192)

International cooperation becomes supremely necessary with respect to those people who, in addition to many other problems, are today often enough burdened in a special way with the difficulties stemming from a rapid population growth. There is urgent need for all nations, especially the richer ones, to cooperate fully and intensely in an exploration as to how there can be prepared and distributed to the human community whatever is required for the livelihood and proper training of men. Some peoples, indeed, would greatly better their conditions of life if they could be duly trained to abandon ancient methods of farming in favor of modern techniques. With necessary prudence they should adapt these techniques to their own situations. In addition they need to establish a better social order and regulate the distribution of land with greater fairness. (GS 87)

Within the limits of their own competence, government officials have rights and duties with regard to the population problems of their own nation, for instance in the matter of social legislation as it affects families, of migration to cities, of information relative to conditions and needs of the nation. Since the minds of men are so powerfully disturbed about this problem, the council also desires that, especially in universities, Catholic experts in all these aspects should skillfully pursue their studies and projects and give them an even wider scope. (GS 87)

Many people assert that it is absolutely necessary for population growth to be radically reduced everywhere or at least in certain nations. They say this must be done by every possible means and by every kind of government intervention. Hence this Council exhorts all to beware against solutions contradicting the moral law, solutions which have been promoted publicly or privately and sometimes actually imposed. (GS 87)

For in view of the inalienable human right to marry and beget children, the question of how many children should be born belongs to the honest judgment of parents. The question can in no way be committed to the decision of government. Now since the judgment of parents supposes a rightly formed conscience, it is highly important that everyone be given the opportunity to practice upright and truly human responsibility. This responsibility respects the divine law and takes account of circumstances and the times. It requires that education and social conditions in various places be changed for the better and especially that religious instruction or at least full moral training be provided. (GS 87)

Human beings should also be judiciously informed of scientific advances in the exploration and methods by which spouses

Social Structures and Functions

can be helped in arranging the number of their children. The reliability of these methods should be adequately proved and their harmony with the moral order should be clear. (GS 87)

As everybody knows, there are countries with an abundance of arable land and a scarcity of manpower, while in other countries there is no proportion between natural resources and the capital available. This demands that peoples should set up relationships of mutual collaboration, facilitating the circulating from one to the other of capital, goods and manpower. (PT 101)

Here we deem it opportune to remark that, whenever possible, the work to be done should be taken to the workers, not vice versa. (PT 102)

In this way a possibility of a better future is offered to many persons without their being forced to leave their own environment in order to seek residence elsewhere, which almost always entails the heartache of separation and difficult periods of adjustment and social integration. (PT 102)

One cannot deny the existence, especially in the southern hemisphere, of a demographic problem which creates difficulties for development. One must immediately add that in the northern hemisphere the nature of this problem is reversed: here the cause of concern is the drop in the birthrate, with repercussions on the aging of the population, unable even to renew itself biologically. In itself, this is a phenomenon capable of hindering development. Just as it is incorrect to say that such difficulties stem solely from demographic growth, neither is it proved that all demographic growth is incompatible with orderly development. (SRS 25)

On the other hand, it is very alarming to governments in many countries launching systematic campaigns against birth, contrary not only to the cultural and religious identity of the countries themselves but also contrary to the nature of true development. It often happens that these campaigns are the result of pressure and financing coming from abroad, and in some cases they are made a condition for the granting of financial and economic aid and assistance. In any event, there is an absolute lack of respect for the freedom of choice of the parties involved, men and women often subjected to intolerable pressures, including economic ones, in order to force them to submit to this new form of oppression. It is the poorest populations which suffer such mistreatment, and this sometimes leads to a tendency toward a form of racism or the promotion of a certain equally racist forms of eugenics. (SRS 25)

Man has a right to leave his native land for various motives—and also the right to return—in order to seek better conditions of life in another country. This fact is certainly not without difficulties of various kinds. Above all, it generally constitutes a loss for the country which is left behind. It is the departure of a person who is also a member of a great community united by history, tradition, and culture, and that person must begin life in the midst of another society united by a different culture and very often by a different language. In this case it is the loss of a subject of work, whose efforts of mind and body could contribute to the common good of his own country, but these efforts, his contributions, are instead offered to another society which in a sense has less right to them than the person's country of origin. (*Laborem Exercens*, LE 23)

Nevertheless, even if emigration is in some aspects an evil, in certain circumstances it is, as the phrase goes, a necessary evil. Everything should be done—and certainly is being done to this end—to prevent this material evil from causing greater moral harm; indeed every possible effort should be made to ensure that it may bring benefit to the emigrant's personal, family, and social life, both to the country to which he goes and the country which he leaves. In this area much depends on just legislation, in particular with regard to the rights of workers. It is obvious that the question of just legislation enters into the context of present considerations, especially from the point of view of these rights. (LE 23)

D. Community and Particular Characteristics

1. Social Unity

God did not create man for a life in isolation but for the formation of social unity. So also "it has pleased God to make men holy and save them not merely as individuals, without any mutual bonds, but by making them into a single people, a people which acknowledges Him in truth and serves Him in holiness" (*Lumen Gentium*, LG 9). So from the beginning of salvation history He has chosen men not just as individuals but as members of a certain community. Revealing His mind to them, God calls those chosen ones "His people" (Exod 3:7-12) and furthermore, made a covenant with them on Sinai. (GS 32)

This communitarian character is developed and consummated in the work of Jesus Christ. For the very Word made flesh willed to share in the human fellowship. He was present at the wedding of Cana, visited the house of Zacchaeus, ate with publicans and sinners. He revealed the love of the Father and the sublime vocation of man in terms of the most common of social realities and by making use of speech and the imagery of plain, everyday life. Willingly obeying the laws of his country, He sanctified those human ties, especially family ones, from which social relationships arise. He chose to lead the life proper to an artisan of His time and place. (GS 32)

Because of changes in the social order, the traditional local communities such as father-centered families, clans, tribes, villages, various groups and associations stemming from social contacts, experience more thorough change every day. (GS 6)

2. Associations

Actually, increased complexity of social life by no means results from a blind drive of natural forces. Indeed, it is the creation of free men who are so disposed to act by nature as to be responsible for what they do. They must, of course, recognize the laws of human progress and the development of economic life and take these into account. Furthermore, men are not altogether free from their milieu. (MM 63)

Accordingly, advances in social organizations can and should be so brought about that maximum advantages accrue to citizens while at the same time disadvantages are averted or at least minimized. (MM 64)

That these desired objectives be more readily obtained, it is necessary that public authorities have a correct understanding of the common good. This embraces the sum total of those conditions of social living, whereby men are enabled more fully and readily to achieve their own perfection. Hence, we regard it as necessary that the various intermediary bodies and the numerous social undertakings wherein an expanded social structure primarily finds expression be ruled by their own laws and, as the common good itself progresses, pursue this objective in a spirit of sincere concord among themselves. Nor is it less necessary that the above-mentioned groups present the form and substance of a true community. This they will do only if individual members are considered and treated as persons and are encouraged to participate in the affairs of the group. (MM 65)

Accordingly, as relationships multiply between men, binding them more closely together, commonwealths will more readily and appropriately order their affairs to the extent these two factors are kept in balance: 1) the freedom of individual citizens and groups of citizens to act autonomously while cooperating one with the other; 2) the activity of the state whereby the undertakings of private individuals and groups are suitably regulated and fostered. (MM 66)

Now if social systems are organized in accord with the above norms and moral laws, their extension does not necessarily mean that individual citizens will be gravely discriminated against or excessively burdened. Rather, we hope that this will enable man not only to develop and perfect his natural talents but also will lead to the appropriate structuring of the human community. Such a structure, as our predecessor of happy memory Pius XI

Social Structures and Functions

warned in his Encyclical Letter *Quadragesimo Anno*, is absolutely necessary for the adequate fulfillment of the rights and duties of social life. (MM 67)

From the fact that human beings are by nature social, there arises the right of assembly and association. They have also the right to give the societies of which they are members the form they consider the most suitable for the aim they have in view and to act within such societies on their own initiative and responsibility in order to achieve their desired objectives. (PT 23)

From the Christian vision of the human person there necessarily follows a correct picture of society. According to *Rerum Novarum* and the whole social doctrine of the church, the social nature of man is not completely fulfilled in the state but is realized in various intermediary groups, beginning with the family and including economic, social, political, and cultural groups which stem from human nature itself and have their own autonomy, always with a view to the common good. This is what I have called the "subjectivity" of society which, together with the subjectivity of the individual, was cancelled out by "Real Socialism." (*Octogesimo Adveniens*, OA 13)

3. Structural Changes in Communities

a. Urbanization

After long centuries, agrarian civilization is weakening. Is sufficient attention being devoted to the arrangement and improvement of the life of the country people, whose inferior and at times miserable economic situation provoke the flight to the unhappy crowded conditions of the city outskirts, where neither employment nor housing awaits them? (OA 8)

This unceasing flight from the land, industrial growth, continual demographic expansion, and the attraction of urban centers bring about concentrations of population, the extent of which is difficult to imagine, for people are already speaking in terms of "megalopolis" grouping together tens of millions of persons. Of course there exist medium-sized towns, the dimension of which assures a better balance in the population. While being able to offer employment to those that progress in agriculture makes available, they permit an adjustment of the human environment which better avoids the proletarianism and crowding of the built-up areas. (OA 8)

Not only had God given the earth to man, who must use it with respect for the original purpose for which it was given to him, but man too is God's gift to man. He must therefore respect the natural and moral structure with which he has been endowed. In this context, mention should be made of the serious problems of modern urbanization, of the need for urban planning which is concerned with how people are to live, and of the attention which should be given to a "social ecology" of work. (CA 38)

b. International Community

Today the bonds of mutual dependence become increasingly close between all citizens and all the peoples of the world. The universal common good needs to be intelligently pursued and more effectively achieved. Hence it is now necessary for the family of nations to create for themselves an order which corresponds to modern obligations, particularly with reference to those numerous regions still laboring under intolerable need. (GS 84)

For the attainment of these goals, agencies of the international community should do their part to provide for the various necessities of men. In the field of social life this means food, health, education, and employment. In certain situations which can obtain anywhere, it means the general need to promote the growth of developing nations, to attend to the hardships of refugees scattered throughout the world, or to assist migrants and their families. (GS 84)

The international agencies, both universal and regional, which already exist assuredly deserve well of the human race. These stand forth as the first attempts to lay international foundations under the whole human community for the solving of the critical problems of our age, the promotion of global progress, and the prevention of any kind of war. The Church rejoices at the spirit of true fraternity flourishing between Christians and non-Christians in all these areas. The spirit strives to see that ever more intense efforts are made for the relief of the world's enormous miseries. (GS 84)

c. Small Christian Communities

These base communities first established through the Latin American Episcopal Conference are intended to foster interrelationships, acceptance of God's word, reflection on reality and the Gospel, to bring families together in intimate relationships grounded in faith, and to embody the church's preferential love for the poor.

4. Common Good

Individuals, families, and various groups which compose the civic community are aware of their own insufficiency in the matter of establishing a fully human condition of life. They see that need for a wider community in which each would daily contribute his energies toward the even better attainment of the common good. It is for this reason they set up the political community in all of its manifold expressions. (GS 74)

Hence the political community exists for the common good in which the community finds its full justification and meaning, and from which it derives its pristine and proper right. Now, the common good embraces the sum of those conditions of social life by which individuals, families, and groups can achieve their own fulfillment in a relatively thorough and ready way. (GS 74)

The common good of man is in its basic sense determined by the eternal law. Still the concrete demands of this common good are constantly changing as time goes on. (GS 78)

Individual citizens and intermediary groups are obliged to make their specific contributions to the common welfare. One of the chief consequences of this is that they must bring their own interests into harmony with the needs of the community and must contribute their goods and their services, as civil authorities have prescribed, in accord with the norms of justice and within the limits of their competence. Clearly then those who wield power in the state must do this by such acts which have not only been carried out but which also either have the common welfare primarily in view or which can lead to it. (PT 53)

Indeed since the whole reason for the existence of civil authorities is the realization of the common good, it is clearly necessary that, in pursuing this objective, they should respect the essential elements and at the same time conform their laws to the circumstances of the day. (PT 54)

Assuredly, the ethnic characteristics of the various human groups are to be respected as constituent elements of the common good. But these characteristics by no means exhaust the content of the common good. For the common good is intimately bound up with human nature. It can never exist fully and completely unless, its intimate nature and realization being what they are, the human person is taken into account. (PT 55)

The very nature of the common good requires that all members of the state be entitled to share in it, although in different ways according to each one's tasks, merits, and circumstances. For this reason, every civil authority must take pains to promote the common good of all, without preference for any single citizen or civic group. As our predecessor of immortal memory Leo XIII has said: "The civil power must not serve the advantage of any one individual, or some few persons, inasmuch as it was established for the common good of all" (*Immortale Dei*). Considerations of justice and equity, however, at times demand that those involved in civil government give more attention to the less fortunate members of the community since they are less able to assert their legitimate claims. (PT 56)

At the present time, no political community is able to pursue its own interests and develop itself in isolation because its prosperity and development are both a reflection and a component part of the prosperity and development of all other political communities. (PT 131)

The unity of the human family has always existed because its members are human beings all equal by virtue of their natural dignity. Hence there will always exist the objective need to promote in sufficient measure the universal common good, that is, the common good of the entire human family. (PT 132)

5. Culture

a. Culture and Authentic Humanity

It is a fact bearing on the very person of man that he can come to an authentic and full humanity only through culture, that is, through the cultivation of natural goods and values. Wherever human life is involved, therefore, nature and culture are quite intimately connected. (GS 53)

The word "culture" in its general sense indicates all those factors by which man refines and unfolds his manifold spiritual and bodily qualities. It means his effort to bring the world under his control by his knowledge and by his labor. It includes the fact that by improving customs and institutions he renders social life more human both within the family and in the civic community. Finally, it is a feature of culture that throughout the course of time man expresses, communicates, and conserves in his works great spiritual experiences and desires so that these may be of advantage to the progress of many, even of the whole human family. (GS 53)

Hence it follows that human culture necessarily has a historical and social aspect and that the word "culture" often takes on a sociological and ethnological sense. It is in this sense that we speak of a plurality of cultures. (GS 53)

Various conditions of community living, as well as various patterns for organizing the goods of life, arise from the diverse ways of using things, of laboring, of expressing oneself, of practicing religion, of forming customs, of establishing laws and juridical institutions, of advancing the arts and sciences, and of promoting beauty. Thus the customs handed down to it form for each human community its proper patrimony. Thus, too, is fashioned the specific historical environment which enfolds the men of every nation and age and from which they draw the values which permit them to promote human civic culture. (GS 53)

All human activity takes place within a culture and interacts with culture. For an adequate formation of a culture, the involvement of the whole man is required, whereby he exercises his creativity, intelligence, and knowledge of the world and of people. Furthermore, he displays his capacity for self-control, solidarity, and a readiness to promote the common good. Thus the first and most important task is accomplished within man's heart. The way in which he is involved in building his own future depends on the understanding he has of himself and his destiny. It is on this level that the Church promotes those aspects of human behavior that favor a true culture of peace, as opposed to models in which the individual is lost in the crowd, in which the role of his initiative and freedom is neglected, and in which his greatness is posited in the arts of conflict and war. (CA 51)

b. Culture and the Gospel

There are many links between the message of salvation and human culture. For God, revealing Himself to His people, to the extent of a full manifestation of Himself in His incarnate Son, has spoken according to the culture proper to the different ages. (GS 58)

Living in various circumstances during the course of time, the Church, too, has used in her preaching the discovery of different cultures to spread and explain the message of Christ to all nations, to probe it and more deeply understand it, and to give it better expression in liturgical celebrations in the life of the diversified community of the faithful. (GS 58).

But at the same time, the Church, sent to all peoples of every time and place, is not bound exclusively and indissolubly to any race or nation, nor to any particular way of life or any customary pattern of living, ancient or recent. Faithful to her own tradition and at the same time conscious of her universal mission, she can enter into communion with various cultural modes, to her enrichment and theirs too. (GS 58)

The good news of Christ constantly renews the life and culture of fallen man. It combats and removes the errors and evils resulting from sinful allurements which are a perpetual threat. It never ceases to purify and elevate the morality of peoples. By enriching them from above, it makes fruitful, as it were from within, the spiritual qualities and gifts of every people and every age. It strengthens, perfects, and restores them in Christ. Thus by the very fulfillment of her mission, the church stimulates and advances human and civic culture. By her action, even in its liturgical form, she leads men toward interior liberty. (GS 58)

May the faithful, therefore, live in very close union with the men of their time. Let them strive to understand perfectly their way of thinking and feeling, as expressed in their culture. Let them blend modern science and its theories and the understanding of the most recent discoveries with Christian morality and doctrine. Thus their religious practice and morality can keep pace with their scientific knowledge and with an ever-advancing technology. Thus too they will be able to test and interpret all things in a truly Christian spirit. (GS 62)

3

Development

Personal and societal development has been a major concern and an area of activity of the church for ages. A more systematic analysis of the issues and a resolve to become even more involved in development began with the Second Vatican Council, followed closely by Pope Paul VI's Encyclical *Populorum Progressio* in 1967 and twenty years later by Pope John Paul II's Encyclical *Sollicitudo Rei Socialis*.

A. Christian Vision

The development of peoples has the Church's close attention, particularly the development of those peoples who are striving to escape from hunger, misery, endemic diseases, and ignorance; of those who are looking for a wider share of the benefits of civilization and a more active improvement of their human qualities; of those who are aiming purposefully at their complete fulfillment. Following the Second Vatican Ecumenical Council, a renewed consciousness of the demands of the Gospel makes it her duty to put herself at the service of all, to help them grasp their serious problem in all of its dimension, and to convince them that their solidarity in action at this turning point in human history is a matter of urgency. (*Populorum Progressio,* PP 1)

Freedom from misery, the greater assurance of finding subsistence, health, and fixed employment; an increased share of responsibility without oppression of any kind and in security from situations that do violence to their dignity as men; better education—in brief, to seek to do more, know more and have more in order to be more: that is what men aspire to now when a greater number of them are condemned to live in conditions that make this lawful desire illusory. Besides, peoples who have recently gained national independence experience the need to add to this political freedom a fitting autonomous growth, social as well as economic, in order to assure their citizens of a full human enhancement and take their rightful place with other nations. (PP 6)

Development cannot be limited to mere economic growth. In order to be authentic, it must be complete, integral; that is, it has to promote the good of every man and of the whole man. As an eminent specialist has very rightly and emphatically declared: "We do not believe in separating the economic from the human, nor development from the civilizations in which it exists. What we hold important is man, each man and each group of men, and we even include the whole of humanity" (L. J. Lebret, OP, *Dynamique Concrete du Developpement*). (PP 14)

In the design of God, every man is called on to develop and fulfill himself, for every life is a vocation. At birth, everyone is granted, in germ, a set of aptitudes and qualities for him to bring to fruition. Coming to maturity, which will be the result of education received from the environment and personal efforts, will allow each man to direct himself toward the destiny intended for him by his Creator. Endowed with intelligence and freedom, he is responsible for his fulfillment as he is for his salvation. He is aided, or sometimes impeded, by those who educate him and those with whom he lives, but each one remains, whatever be these influences affecting him, the principal agent of his own success or failure. By the unaided effort of his own intelligence and his will, each man can grow in his humanity, can enhance his personal worth, can become more a person. (PP 15)

"Fill the earth and subdue it" (Gen 1:28): the Bible, from the first page on, teaches us that the whole of creation is for man and that it is his responsibility to develop it by intelligent effort and by means of his labor to perfect it, so to speak, for his use. If the world is made to furnish each individual with the means of livelihood and the instruments for his growth and progress, each man has therefore the right to find in the world what is necessary for himself. The recent Council reminds us of this: God intended the earth and all that it contains for the use of every human being and people. Thus, as all men follow justice and unite in charity, created goods should abound for them on a reasonable basis. All other rights whatsoever, including those of property and of free commerce, are to be subordinated to this principle. They should not hinder but on the contrary favor its application. It is a grave and urgent social duty to redirect them to their primary finality. (PP 22)

We do not know the time for the consummation of the earth and of humanity. Nor do we know how all things will be transformed. As deformed by sin, the shape of this world will pass away. But we are taught that God is preparing a new dwelling place and a new earth where justice will abide and whose blessedness will answer and surpass all the longings for peace which spring up in the human heart. (GS 39)

Then, with death overcome, the sons of God will be raised up in Christ. What was sown in weakness and corruption will be clothed in incorruptibility. While charity and its fruits endure, all that creation which God made on man's account will be unchained from the bondage of vanity (GS 39).

Therefore, while we are warned that it profits a man nothing if he gains the whole world and loses himself, the expectation of a new earth must not weaken but rather stimulate our concern for cultivating this one. For here grows the body of a new human family, a body which even now is able to give some kind of foreshadowing of the new age. (GS 39)

Earthly progress must be carefully distinguished from the growth of Christ's kingdom. Nevertheless, to the extent that the former can contribute to the better ordering of human society, it is of vital concern to the kingdom of God. (GS 39)

For after we have obeyed the Lord and in His Spirit nurtured on earth the values of human dignity, brotherhood, and freedom, and indeed all the good fruits of our nature and enterprise, we will find them again but freed from stain, burnished, and transfigured. This will be so when Christ hands over to the Father a kingdom eternal and universal: "a kingdom of truth and life, or holiness and grace, or justice, love and peace" (Preface of the Feast of Christ the King). On this earth that kingdom is already present in mystery. When the Lord returns, it will be brought into full flower. (GS 39)

The economy has as its objective the development of wealth and its progressive increase, not only in quantity but also in quality; this is morally correct if it is directed to man's overall development in solidarity and to that of the society in which people live and work. Development, in fact, cannot be reduced to a mere process of accumulating goods and services. On the contrary, accumulation by itself, even if it were for the common good, is not a sufficient condition for bringing about authentic human happiness. In this sense, the church's social magisterium warns against the treachery hidden within a development that is only quantitative, for the excessive availability of every kind of material for the benefit of certain social groups, easily makes people slaves of possession and immediate gratification. This is the so-called civilization of consumption or consumerism. (*Compendium of the Social Doctrine of the Church*, CSDC 334)

B. Urgency and Fullness of Development

Man's creative activity, his intelligence and his work, have brought about profound changes both in the field of sciences and technology and in that of social and cultural life. Man has extended his power over nature and has acquired deeper knowledge of the laws of social behavior. He has seen the obstacles and distances between individuals and nations dissolve or shrink through an increased sense of what is universal, through a clearer awareness of the unity of the human race, through the acceptance of mutual dependence in authentic solidarity, and through the desire and possibility of making contact with one's brothers and sisters beyond artificial geographical divisions and national or racial limits. Today's young people, especially, know that the progress of science and technology can produce not only new material goods but also a wider sharing in knowledge. The extraordinary progress made in the field of information and data processing, for instance, will increase man's creative capacity and provide access to the intellectual and cultural riches of other people. New communications techniques will encourage participation in events and a wider exchange of ideas. The achievement of biological, psychological, and social sciences will help man to understand better the riches of his own being. It is true that too often this progress is still the privilege of the industrialized countries, but it cannot be denied that the prospect of enabling every country to benefit from it has long ceased to be a mere utopia when there is a real political desire for it. (*Dives in Misericordia*, DM 10)

We must make haste: too many are suffering, and the distance is growing that separates the progress of some and the stagnation, not to say regression, of others. Yet the work required should advance smoothly if there is not to be the risk of losing indispensable equilibrium. A hasty agrarian reform can fail. Industrialization if introduced suddenly can displace structures still necessary and produce hardships in society which would be a setback in terms of human values. (PP 29)

There are certainly situations whose injustice cries to heaven. When whole populations destitute of necessities live in a state of dependence barring them from all initiative and responsibility and all opportunity to advance culturally and share in social and political life, recourse to violence, as a means to right these wrongs to human dignity, is a grave temptation. (PP 30)

We know, however, that a revolutionary uprising—save where there is manifest, long-standing tyranny which would

Development

do great damage to fundamental human rights and dangerous harm to the common good of the country—produces new injustices, throws more elements out of balance and brings on new disasters. A real evil should not be fought against at the cost of greater misery. (PP 31)

We want to be clearly understood: the present situation must be faced with courage and the injustices linked with it must be fought against and overcome. Development demands bold transformations, innovations that go deep. Urgent reforms should be undertaken without delay. It is for each one to take his share in them with generosity, particularly those whose education, position, and opportunities afford them wide scope for action. May they show an example and give of their own possessions as several of our brothers in the episcopacy have done. In so doing they will live up to men's expectations and be faithful to the Spirit of God, since it is the ferment of the Gospel which has aroused and continues to arouse in man's heart the irresistible requirements of his dignity. (PP 32)

It can be affirmed that economic growth depends in the very first place upon social progress; thus basic education is the primary object of any plan of development. Indeed, hunger for education is no less debasing than hunger for food: an illiterate is a person with an undernourished mind. To be able to read and write, to acquire a professional formation, means to recover confidence in oneself and to discover that one can make progress along with the others. We also rejoice at the good work accomplished in this field by private initiative, by the public authorities, and by international organizations; these are the primary agents of development because they render man capable of acting for himself. (PP 35)

But man finds his true identity only in his social milieu, where the family plays a fundamental role. The family's influence may have been excessive to the detriment of the fundamental rights of the individual. The longstanding social frameworks, often too rigid and badly organized, existing in developing countries, are, nevertheless, still necessary for a time, yet progressively relaxing their excessive hold on the population. But the natural family, monogamous and stable, such as the divine plan conceived it and as Christianity sanctified it, must remain the place where "the various generations come together and help one another to grow wiser and to harmonize personal rights with the other requirements of social life" (GS 52). (PP 36)

Excessive economic, social, and cultural inequalities among peoples arouse tensions and conflicts and are a danger to peace. As we said to the Fathers of the Council when we returned from our journey of peace to the United Nations: "The condition of the peoples in process of development ought to be the object of our consideration; or better: our charity for the poor in the world—and there are multitudes of them—must become more considerate, more active, more generous." To wage war on misery and to struggle against injustice is to promote, along with improved conditions, the human and spiritual progress of all men and therefore the common good of humanity. Peace cannot be limited to a mere absence of war, the result of an ever-precarious balance of forces. No, peace is something that is built up day after day in pursuit of an order intended by God which implies a more perfect form of justice among men. (PP 76)

The people themselves have the prime responsibility to work for their own development. But they will not bring this about in isolation. Regional agreements among weak nations for mutual support, understanding of wider scope entered into for their help, more far-reaching agreements to establish programs for closer cooperation among groups of nations—these are the milestones on the road to development that lead to peace. (PP 77)

In the fields of science, technology, and economics, these developments are especially worthy of note: the discovery of atomic energy, employed first for military purposes and later increasingly for peaceful ends, the almost limitless possibilities opened up by chemistry in synthetic products, the growth of automation in the sectors of industry and services, the modernization of agriculture, the nearly complete conquest especially through radio and television of the distance separating peoples, the greatly increased speed of all manner of transportation, the initial conquest of outer space. (MM 47)

Turning to the social field, the following contemporary trends are evident: development of systems for social insurance, the introduction of social security in some more affluent countries, and greater awareness among workers as members of unions of the principal issues in economic and social life, a progressive improvement of basic education, wider diffusion among the citizenry of the conveniences of life, increased social mobility and a resulting decline in division among the classes, greater interest than heretofore in world affairs on the part of those with average education. Meanwhile, if one considers the social and economic advances made in a growing number of countries, he will quickly discern increasingly pronounced imbalances: first between agriculture on the one hand and industry and the services on the other, between the more and the less developed regions within countries, and finally on a worldwide scale between countries with differing economic resources and development. (MM 48)

Turning now to political affairs, it is evident that here, too, a number of innovations have occurred. Today, in many communities, citizens from almost all social strata participate in public life. Public authorities intervene more and more in economic and social affairs. The peoples of Asia and Africa, having set aside colonial systems, now govern themselves according to their own laws and institutions. As mutual relationships of peoples increase, they become daily more dependent one upon the other. Throughout the world, assemblies and councils have become more common which, being supranational in character, take into account the interests of all peoples. Such bodies are concerned with economic life or with social affairs or with culture and education or, finally, with the mutual relationships of peoples. (MM 49)

C. Development, Wealthy and Developing Nations

The world is sick. Its illness consists less in the unproductive monopolization of resources by a small number of men than in the lack of brotherhood among individuals and peoples. (PP 66)

There can be no progress toward the complete development of man without the simultaneous development of all humanity in the spirit of solidarity. As we said at Bombay: "Man must meet man, nation meet nation, as brothers and sisters, as children of God. In this mutual understanding and friendship, in this sacred communion, we must also begin to work together to build the common future of the human race." We also suggested a search for concrete and practical ways of organization and cooperation so that all available resources be pooled and thus a true communion among all nations be achieved. (PP 43)

This duty is the concern especially of better-off nations. Their obligations stem from a brotherhood that is at once human and supernatural and take on a threefold aspect: the duty of solidarity, the aid that the rich nations must give to developing countries; the duty of social justice, the rectification of inequitable trade relations between powerful nations and weak nations; the duty of universal charity, the effort to bring about a world that is more human toward all men, where all will be able to give and receive without one group making progress at the expense of the other. The question is urgent, for on it depends the future of the civilization of the world. (PP 44)

We must repeat once more that the superfluous wealth of rich countries should be placed at the service of poor nations. The rule, which up to now held good for the benefit of those nearest to us, must today be applied to all the needy of this world. Besides, the rich will be the first to benefit as a result. Otherwise their continued greed will certainly call down upon them the judgment of God and the wrath of the poor with consequences no one can foretell. If today's flourishing civilizations remain selfishly wrapped up in themselves, they could easily place their highest values in jeopardy, sacrificing their will to be great to the desire to possess more. To them we could also apply the parable of the rich man whose fields yielded an abundant harvest and who did not know where to store his harvest: "God said to him: 'Fool, this night do they demand your soul of you'" (Luke 12:20). (PP 49)

There is certainly no need to do away with bilateral and multilateral agreements: they allow ties of dependence and feelings of bitterness, left over from the era of colonialism, to yield place to the happier relationships of friendship based on a footing of constitutional and political equality. However, if they were to be fitted into the framework of worldwide collaboration, they would be beyond all suspicion, and as a result, there would be less distrust on the part of the receiving nations. These would have less cause for fearing that under the cloak of financial aid or technical assistance there lurk certain manifestations of what has come to be called neocolonialism, in the form of political pressures and economic suzerainty aimed at maintaining or acquiring complete dominance. (PP 52)

Anguished appeals have already been sounded in the past; that of John XXIII was warmly received. We ourselves have repeated it in our Christmas message of 1963 and again in 1966 on behalf of India. The campaign against hunger being carried on by the Food and Agriculture Organization (FAO) and encouraged by the Holy See has been generously supported. Our Caritas Internationalism is at work everywhere, and many Catholics, at the urging of our brothers in the episcopacy, contribute generously of their means and spend themselves without counting the cost in assisting those who are in want, continually widening the circle of those they look upon as neighbors. (PP 46)

But neither all of this nor the private and public funds that have been invested nor the gifts and loans that have been made can suffice. It is not just a matter of eliminating hunger, or even reducing poverty. The struggle against destitution, though urgent and necessary, is not enough. It is a question, rather, of building a world where every man, no matter what his race, religion, or nationality, can live a fully human life, freed from servitude imposed on him by other men or by natural forces over which he has not sufficient control, a world where freedom is not an empty word and where the poor man Lazarus can sit down at the same table with the rich man. This demands great generosity, much sacrifice, and unceasing effort on the part of the rich man. Let each one examine his conscience, a conscience that conveys a new message for our times. Is he prepared to support out of his own pocket works and undertakings organized in favor of the most destitute? Is he prepared to pay higher taxes so that the public authorities can intensify their efforts in favor of development? Is he prepared to pay a higher price for imported goods so that the producer may be more justly rewarded? Or to leave his country, if necessary and he is young, in order to assist in this development of the young nations? (PP 47)

D. Development, Constant and Changing, Failures and Successes

I (Pope John Paul II) wish principally to achieve two objectives of no little importance: on the one hand to pay homage to this historic document of Paul VI (*Populorum Progressio*) and to its teaching; on the other hand, following in the footsteps of my esteemed predecessors in the See of Peter, to reaffirm the continuity of the social doctrine as well as its constant renewal. In effect, continuity and renewal are a proof of the perennial value of the teaching of the church. (SRS 3)

This twofold dimension is typical of her teaching in the social sphere. On the one hand, it is constant, for it remains identical in its fundamental inspiration, in its "principles of reflection," in its "criteria of judgment," in its basic "directives for action," and above all in its vital link with the Gospel of the Lord. On the other hand, it is ever new, because it is subject to the necessary and opportune adaptations suggested by the changes in historical conditions and by the unceasing flow of events which are the setting of the life of people and society. (SRS 3)

Development

In its own time, the fundamental teaching of the encyclical *Populorum Progressio* received great acclaim for its novel character. The social context in which we live today cannot be said to be completely identical with that of twenty years ago. (SRS 11)

The first fact to note is the hopes for development, at that time so lively, appear today very far from being realized. In this regard, the encyclical had no illusions. Its language, grave and at times dramatic, limited itself to stressing the seriousness of the situation and to bring before the conscience of all the urgent obligation of contributing to its solution. In those years there was a certain widespread optimism about the possibility of overcoming, without excessive efforts, the economic backwardness of the poorer peoples, of providing them with infrastructures and assisting them in the process of industrialization. (SRS 12)

The abundance of goods and services available in some parts of the world, particularly in the developed North, is matched in the South by an unacceptable delay, and it is precisely in this geopolitical area that the major part of the human race lives. (SRS 14)

Looking at all of the various sectors—the production and distribution of foodstuffs, hygiene, health and housing, availability of drinking water, working conditions (especially for women), life expectancy, and other economic and social indicators—the general picture is a disappointing one, both considered in itself and in relation to the corresponding data of the more developed countries. The word "gap" returns spontaneously to mind. (SRS 14)

Perhaps this is not the appropriate word for indicating the true reality, since it gives the impression of a stationary phenomenon. This is not the case. The pace of progress in the developed and developing countries in recent years has differed, and this serves to widen the distances. Thus the developing countries, especially the poorest of them, find themselves in a situation of very serious delay. (SRS 14)

We must also add the difference of culture and value systems between the various population groups, differences which do not always match the degree of economic development but which help to create distances. These are elements and aspects which render the social question much more complex, precisely because this question has assumed a universal dimension. (SRS 14)

However, the picture just given would be incomplete if one failed to add to the "economic and social indices" of underdevelopment other indices which are equally negative and indeed even more disturbing, beginning with the cultural level. These are illiteracy; the difficulty or impossibility of obtaining higher education; the inability to share in the building of one's own nation; the various forms of exploitation and of economic, social, political and even religious oppression of the individual and his or her rights; discrimination of every type, especially the exceptionally odious form based on difference of race. If some of these scourges are noted with regret in areas of the more developed North, they are undoubtedly more frequent, more lasting, and more difficult to root out in the developing and less advanced countries. (SRS 15)

However much society worldwide shows signs of fragmentation, expressed in the conventional names First, Second, Third, and even Fourth World, their interdependence remains close. When this interdependence is separated from its ethical requirements, it has disastrous consequences for the weakest. Indeed, as a result of a sort of internal dynamic and under the impulse of mechanisms which can only be called perverse, this interdependence triggers negative effects even in the rich countries. It is precisely within these countries that one encounters, though on a lesser scale, the more specific manifestations of underdevelopment. Thus it should be obvious the development either becomes shared by every part of the world or it undergoes a process of regression even in zones marked by constant progress. This tells us a great deal about the nature of authentic development: either all the nations of the world participate or it will not be true development. (SRS 17)

The first specific sign of underdevelopment is the housing crisis. Another indicator common to the vast majority of nations is the phenomenon of unemployment and underemployment. A third phenomenon, likewise characteristic of the most recent period, even though it is not met everywhere, is without doubt equally indicative of the interdependence between developed and less developed countries. It is the question of international debt. (SRS 17–19)

If arms production is a serious disorder in the present world with regard to true human needs and the employment of means capable of satisfying those needs, the arms trade is equally to blame. Indeed, with reference to the latter it must be added that the moral judgment is even more severe. As we all know, this is a trade without frontiers, capable of crossing even the barriers of the blocs. It knows how to overcome the division between East and West, and above all the one between North and South, to the point—and this is more serious—of pushing its way into the different sections which make up the southern hemisphere. We are thus confronted with a strange phenomenon: while economic aid and development plans meet with the obstacle of insuperable ideological barriers and with tariff and trade barriers, arms of whatever origin circulate with almost total freedom all over the world. (SRS 24)

One cannot deny the existence, especially in the southern hemisphere, of a demographic problem which creates difficulties for development. One must immediately add that in the northern hemisphere the nature of the problem is reversed: here, the cause for concern is the drop in birthrate, with repercussions on the aging of the population, unable even to renew itself biologically. In itself, this is a phenomenon capable of hindering development. Just as it is incorrect to say that such difficulties stem solely from demographic growth, neither is it proved that all demographic growth is incompatible with orderly development. (SRS 25)

This mainly negative view of the actual situation of development in the contemporary world would be incomplete without a mention of the coexistence of positive aspects. To be mentioned here, as a sign of respect for life—despite all the temptations to destroy it by abortion and euthanasia—is a concomitant concern for peace, together with an awareness that peace is indivisible. It is for all or none. It demands an even greater degree of rigorous respect for justice and consequently a fair distribution of the results of true development. (SRS 26)

Among today's positive signs we must also mention a greater realization of the limits of available resources and of the need to respect the integrity of the cycles of nature and to take them into account when planning for development, rather than sacrificing them to certain demagogic ideas about the latter. Today this is called ecological concern. (SRS 26)

It is also right to acknowledge the generous commitment of statesmen, politicians, economists, trade unionists, people of science, and international officials—many of them inspired by religious faith—who at no small personal sacrifice try to resolve the world's ills and who give of themselves in every way so as to ensure that an ever increasing number of people may enjoy the benefits of peace and a quality of life worthy of the name. (SRS 26)

The great international organizations, and a number of the regional organizations, contribute to this in no small measure. Their united efforts make possible more effective action. (SRS 26)

It is also through these contributions that some thirdworld countries, despite the burden of many negative factors, have succeeded in reaching a certain self-sufficiency in food or a degree of industrialization which makes it possible to survive with dignity and to guarantee sources of employment for the active population. (SRS 26)

Thus, all is not negative in the contemporary world, nor would it be, for the heavenly Father's providence lovingly watches over even our daily cares. Indeed, the positive values which we have mentioned testify to a new moral concern, particularly with respect to the great human problems such as development and peace. (SRS 26)

The Church's social doctrine holds that authentically human social relationships of friendship, solidarity, and reciprocity can also be conducted within economic activity and not only outside it or "after" it. The economic sphere is neither ethically neutral nor inherently inhuman and opposed to society. It is part and parcel of human activity, and precisely because it is human, it must be structured and governed in an ethical manner. (CV 36)

E. Theological Dimensions

In a document of a pastoral nature such as this, an analysis limited exclusively to the economic and social causes of underdevelopment (and mutatis mutandis, of so-called super-development) would be incomplete. It is therefore necessary to single out the moral causes which, with respect to the behavior of individuals considered as responsible persons, interfere in such a way as to slow down the course of development and hinder its full achievement. (SRS 35)

Similarly, when the scientific and technical resources are available which, with the necessary concrete political decisions, ought to help lead peoples to true development will it be overcome only by means of essentially moral decisions. For believers, and especially for Christians, these decisions will take their inspiration from the principles of faith, with the help of divine grace. (SRS 35)

It is important to note, therefore, that a world which is divided into blocs, sustained by rigid ideologies, and in which instead of interdependence and solidarity different forms of imperialism hold sway, can only be a world subject to structures of sin. The sum total of the negative factors working against a true awareness of the universal common good and the need to further it, gives the impression of creating, in persons and institutions, an obstacle which is difficult to overcome. (SRS 36)

If the present situation can be attributed to difficulties of various kinds, it is not out of place to speak of "structures of sin," which, as I stated in my apostolic exhortation *Reconciliatio et Paenitentia*, are rooted in personal sin and thus always linked to the concrete acts of individuals who introduce these structures, consolidate them, and make them difficult to remove. And thus they grow stronger, spread, and become the source of other sins and so influence people's behavior. (SRS 36)

One can actually speak of "selfishness" and "shortsightedness," of "mistaken political calculations" and "imprudent economic decisions." And in each of these evaluations one hears an echo of an ethical and moral nature. Man's condition is such that a more profound analysis of individual's actions and omissions cannot be achieved without implying, in one way or another, judgments or references of an ethical nature. (SRS 36)

This general analysis, which is religious in nature, can be supplemented by a number of particular considerations to demonstrate that among the actions and attitudes opposed to the will of God, the good of neighbor and the "structures" created by them, two are very typical: on the one hand, the all-consuming desire for profit, and on the other, the thirst for power, with the intention of imposing one's will on others. In order to characterize better each of these attitudes, one can add the expression: "at any price." In other words, we are faced with the absolutizing of human attitudes with all of its possible consequences. (SRS 37)

In the context of these reflections, the decision to set out on or to continue the journey involves, above all, a moral value which men and women of faith recognize as a demand of God's will, the only true foundation of an absolutely binding ethic. (SRS 38)

One would hope also that men and women without an explicit faith would be convinced that the obstacles to integral development are not only economic but rest on more profound attitude which human beings can make into absolute values. Thus one would hope that all those who, to some degree or other, are responsible for ensuring a "more human life" for their fellow human beings, whether or not they are inspired by a religious faith, will become fully aware of the urgent need to change the spiritual attitudes which define each individual's relation with self, with neighbor, with even the remotest human communities, and with nature itself, and all of this in view of higher values such as the common good or, to quote the felicitous expression of the encyclical *Polulorum Progressio*, the full development "of the whole individual and of all people." (SRS 38)

4
Economic Justice

THE CHURCH, IN SEARCH for truth in the social order and for justice between individual persons, institutions, and societies, threw its spiritual and intellectual forces into the study of economic morality. In 1891, Pope Leo XIII gave the world the *Rerum Novarum*, the seed out of which sprang the memorable social papal encyclicals, now for more than a hundred years.

In Leo's time major economic systems were out of control and causing widespread suffering. Unbridled capitalism was dehumanizing countless persons. Its economic opposite, socialism, was gaining strength and under its most radical movement, Marxist Communism, was heading for a revolutionary clash. In the interest of God's people who were the victims of both of these economic systems, Leo forged principles of economic justice which since then have been continually developed by the church under the guidance of the Spirit.

A. Growing Awareness of God-Given, Rational Ideas of Justice in the Economy

1. Development of the Church's Teaching

The "new things" to which the pope devoted his attention were anything but positive. The first paragraph of the encyclical describes in strong terms the "new things" (*rerum novarum*) which gave it its name. "That spirit of revolutionary change which has long been disturbing the nations of the world should have passed beyond the sphere of politics and made its influence felt in the related sphere of practical economics is not surprising. Progress in industry, the development of new trades, the changing relationship between employers and workers, the enormous wealth of a few as opposed to the poverty of the many, the increasing self-reliance of the workers and their association with each other, as well as a notable decline in morality: all these elements have led to the conflict now taking place" (*Rerum Novarum*, RN 128). (CA 5)

Today at a distance of a hundred years, the validity of this approach affords me the opportunity to contribute to the development of Christian social doctrine. The "new evangelization," which the modern world urgently needs and which I have emphasized many times, must include among its essential elements a proclamation of the Church's social doctrine. As in the days of Pope Leo XIII, this doctrine is still suitable for indicating the right way to respond to the great challenges of today, when ideologies are being increasingly discredited. Now, as then, we need to repeat that there can be no genuine solution to the "social question" apart from the Gospel and that the "new things" can find in the Gospel the context for their correct understanding and the proper moral perspective for judgment on them. (CA 5)

As is generally known, in those days an opinion widely prevailed and was commonly put into practice, according to which, in economic matters, everything was to be attributed to inescapable natural forces. Hence, it was held that no connection existed between economic and moral laws. Wherefore, those engaged in economic activity need look no further than their own gain.

Economic Justice

Consequently, mutual relations between economic agents could be left to the play of free and unregulated competition. Interest on capital, prices of goods and services, and profits and wages were to be determined purely mechanically by the laws of the marketplace. Every precaution was to be taken lest the civil authority intervene in any way in economic affairs. During the era, trade unions, according to circumstances in different countries, were sometimes forbidden, sometimes tolerated, sometimes recognized in private law. (MM 11)

Thus, at that time, not only was the proud rule of the stronger recognized as legitimate, so far as economic affairs were concerned, but also prevailed in concrete relations between men. Accordingly, the order of economic affairs was, in general, radically disturbed. (MM 12)

In the encyclical letter of Pius XI *Quadragesimo Anno* (QA), the supreme pontiff first of all confirmed the right and duty of the Catholic Church to make its special contribution in resolving the more serious problems of society which call for the full cooperation of all. Then he reaffirmed those principles and directives of Leo XIII's letter related to the conditions of the times. Finally, he took this occasion not only to clarify certain points of doctrine on which even Catholics were in doubt, but he also showed how the principles and directives themselves regarding social affairs should be adapted to the changing times. (MM 28)

In the message, the great pontiff (Pius XII in 1941) claimed for the Church "the indisputable competence" to "decide whether the basis of a given social system is in accord with the unchangeable order which God our Creator and Redeemer has fixed both in the natural law and revelation." He noted that the letter of Leo XIII is of permanent value and has rich and abiding usefulness. He takes the occasion "to explain in greater detail what the Catholic Church teaches regarding the three principal issues of social life in economic affairs, which are mutually related and connected one with the other and thus interdependent: namely, the use of material goods, labor, and the family" (MM 42).

Concerning the use of material goods, our predecessor declared that the right of every man to use them for his own sustenance is prior to all other rights in economic life, and hence it is prior even to the right of private ownership. It is certain, however, as our predecessor noted, that the right of private property is from the natural law itself. Nevertheless, it is the will of God the Creator that this right to own property should in no way obstruct the flow of "material goods created by God to meet the needs of all men, to all equitably, as justice and charity require." (MM 43)

Whereas in our own era the economies of various countries are evolving very rapidly, more especially since the last great war, we take this opportunity to draw the attention of all to a strict demand of social justice, which explicitly requires that, with the growth of the economy, there occurs a corresponding social development. Thus, all classes of citizens will benefit equitably from an increase in national wealth. Toward this end, vigilance should be exercised and effective steps taken that class differences arising from disparity of wealth not be increased but lessened so far as possible. (MM 73)

2. Process of Economic Development and God's Kingdom

In the socioeconomic realm, the dignity and total vocation of the human person must be honored and advanced along with the welfare of society as a whole. For man is the source, the center, and the purpose of all socioeconomic life. (GS 63)

As in other areas of social life, modern economy is marked by man's increasing domination of nature, by closer and more intense relationships between citizens, groups, and countries and by their mutual dependence, and by more frequent intervention on the part of government. At the same time, progress in the methods of production and in the exchange of goods and services has made the economy an apt instrument for meeting the intensified needs of the human family more successfully. (GS 63)

Today more than ever before, progress in the production of agricultural and industrial goods and in the rendering of services

Economic Justice

is rightly aimed at making provision for the growth of a people and at meeting the rising expectations of the human race. Therefore, technical progress must be fostered, along with a spirit of initiative and eagerness to create and expand enterprises, the adaptation of methods of production—in a word, all the elements making for such development. (GS 64)

The fundamental purpose of this productivity must not be the mere multiplication of products. It must not be profit or domination. Rather, it must be the service of man, and indeed of the whole man, viewed in terms of his material needs and the demands of his intellectual, moral, spiritual, and religious life. And when we say man, we mean every man whatsoever and every group of men, whatever race and from whatever part of the world. Consequently, economic activity is to be carried out according to its own methods and laws but within the limits of morality so that God's plan for mankind can be realized. (GS 64)

Economic development must be kept under the control of mankind. It must not be left to the sole judgment of a few men or groups possessing excessive economic power or of a political community alone or of certain especially powerful nations. It is proper, on the contrary, that at every level the largest possible number of people have an active share in directing that development. When it is a question of international development, all nations should so participate. It is also necessary for the spontaneous activities of individuals and of independent groups to be coordinated with the efforts of public authorities. These activities and these efforts should be aptly and harmoniously interwoven. (GS 65)

Citizens, for their part, should remember that they have the right and the duty, which must be recognized by civil authority, to contribute according to their ability to the true progress of their own community. Especially in underdeveloped areas where resources must be put to urgent use, those men gravely endanger the public good who allow their resources to remain unproductive or who deprive their community of the material and spiritual aid it needs. The personal right of migration, however, is not to be impugned. (GS 65)

Christians who take an active part in modern socioeconomic development and defend justice and charity should be convinced that they can make a great contribution to the prosperity of mankind and the peace of the world. Whether they do so as individuals or in association, let their example be a shining one. After acquiring whatever skills and experience are absolutely necessary, they should in faithfulness to Christ and the Gospel observe the right order of values in their earthly activities. Thus, their whole lives, both individual and social, will be permeated with the spirit of the beatitudes, notable with the spirit of poverty. (GS 72)

Whoever in obedience to Christ seeks first the kingdom of God will as a consequence receive a stronger and purer love for helping all his brothers and for perfecting the work of justice under the inspiration of charity. (GS 72)

3. Common Purpose of All Things

God intended the earth and all that it contains for the use of every human being and people. Thus, as all men follow justice and unite in charity, created goods should abound for them on a reasonable basis. Whatever the forms of ownership may be, as adopted to legitimate institutions of people according to diverse and changeable circumstances, attention must always be paid to the universal purpose for which created goods were meant. In using them, therefore, a man should regard his lawful possessions not merely as his own but also as common property in the sense that they should accrue to the benefit not only of himself but of others. (GS 69)

The distribution of goods should be directed toward providing employment and sufficient income for the people of today and the future. Whether individuals, groups, or public authorities make the decision concerning this distribution and the planning of the economy, they are bound to keep these objectives in mind. They must realize their serious obligation of seeing to it that provision is made for the necessities of a decent life on the part of individuals and of the whole community. They must also look out

Economic Justice

for the future and establish a proper balance between the needs of present-day consumption, both individual and collective, and the necessity of distributing goods on behalf of the coming generation. They should also bear constantly in mind the urgent needs of underdeveloped countries and regions. In financial transactions they should beware of hurting the welfare of their own country or of other countries. Care should be taken lest the economically weak countries unjustly suffer loss from a change in the value of money. (GS 70)

Ownership and other forms of private control over material goods contribute to the expression of personality. Moreover, they furnish men with an occasion for exercising their role in society and in the economy. Hence, it is very important to facilitate the access of both individuals and communities to some control over material goods. (GS 71)

Private ownership or some other kind of dominion over material goods provides everyone with a wholly necessary area of independence and should be regarded as an extension of human freedom. Finally, since it adds incentives for carrying on one's function and duty, it constitutes a kind of prerequisite for civil liberties. (GS 71)

If certain landed estates impede the general prosperity because they are extensive, unused, or poorly used or because they bring hardship to peoples or are detrimental to the interests of the country, the common good sometimes demands their expropriation. While giving a clear statement on this, the Council recalled no less clearly that the available revenue is not to be used in accordance with mere whim and that no place must be given to selfish speculation. Consequently, it is unacceptable that citizens with abundant incomes from the resources and activity of their country should transfer a considerable part of this income abroad purely for their own advantage, without care for the manifest wrong they inflict on their country by doing this. (PP 24)

We consider that we must also stress the new worldwide preoccupation which will be dealt with for the first time in the conference on the human environment to be held in Stockholm in

June 1972. It is impossible to see what right the richer nations have to keep up their claim to increase their own material demands if the consequence is either that others remain in misery or that the danger of destroying the very physical foundations of life on earth is precipitated. Those who are already rich are bound to accept a less material way of life, with less waste, in order to avoid the destruction of the heritage which they are obliged by absolute justice to share with the other members of the human race. (JW 70)

4. The Economy and Public Involvement: Subsidiarity

Growth must not be allowed to follow a kind of automatic course resulting from the economic activity of individuals. Nor must it be entrusted solely to the authority of government. Hence, theories which obstruct the necessary reforms in the name of false liberty must be branded as erroneous. The same is true of those theories which subordinate the basic rights of individual persons and groups to the collective organization of production. (GS 65)

This intervention of public authorities that encourages, stimulates, regulates, supplements, and complements, is based on the principle of subsidiarity, as set forth by Pius XI in his encyclical *Quadragesimo Anno*: "It is a fundamental principle of social philosophy, fixed and unchangeable, that one should not withdraw from individuals and commit to the community what they can accomplish by their own enterprise and industry. So, too, it is an injustice and at the same time a grave evil and a disturbance of right order, to transfer to the larger and higher collectivity functions that can be performed and provided for by lesser and subordinate bodies. Inasmuch as every social activity should, by its very nature, prove a help to members of the body social, it should never destroy or absorb them" (QA 79). (MM 53).

Furthermore, the course of events thus far makes it clear that there cannot be a prosperous and well-ordered society unless both private citizens and public authorities work together in economic affairs. Their activity should be characterized by mutual and amicable efforts, so that the roles assigned to each fit in with

Economic Justice

requirements of the common good as changing times and circumstances suggest. (MM 56)

Experience, in fact, shows that where private initiative of individuals is lacking, political tyranny prevails. Moreover, much stagnation occurs in various sectors of the economy, and hence all sorts of consumer goods and services, closely connected with needs of the body and more especially of the spirit, are in short supply. Beyond doubt, the attainment of such goods and services provides remarkable opportunity and stimulus for individuals to exercise initiative and industry. (MM 57)

Where, on the other hand, appropriate activity of the state is lacking or defective, commonwealths are apt to experience incurable disorders, and there occurs exploitation of the weak by the unscrupulous strong who flourish, unfortunately, like cockle among the wheat, in all times and places. (MM 58)

It is desirable, moreover, that economic development of commonwealths proceed in orderly fashion, meanwhile preserving appropriate balance between the various sectors of the economy. (MM 128)

B. Public, Private Ownership

Over the ages, nearly all societies have provided for both public and private ownership of the goods of the earth. Associated with ownership is the right to determine how and in whose interest the products of the earth, generally resulting from human labor, are to be employed.

Economists explain the source of these products as: 1) *capital*: land, equipment, financial resources, for example, and 2) *labor*: skilled and unskilled, manual, intellectual, and artistic. Societies experience continuing tension, affected by changing circumstances and socioeconomic-political shifts, over how much of a given product belongs to capital, usually represented by owners and managers, how much to workers, and how much to the general welfare of society claimed by such means as taxes.

Tension between the claims of capital and labor, for instance in deciding wages in the private sector, is the subject of labor management negotiations. In the public sector, the state, represented by various agencies of government, is management, and so political forces play a major role in deciding such issues as teachers' salaries. Tensions between these forces are intended to be reduced and the good order of society maintained by labor laws enacted to protect the legitimate interests of labor, management and society itself.

On a more basic and somewhat theoretical level, socioeconomicpolitical tensions have existed over the ages between the claims of private/public ownership and control of property. Private ownership underlies capitalism, public ownership socialism. These opposing systems are seldom found today in their absolute form: totally liberal or laissez-faire capitalism which denies any form of societal control in economic matters and, on the other side, Marxist Communism which eliminates any private ownership and places economic control directly in the hands of the people, represented by the state.

The socioeconomic-political system of today's nations might be characterized as capitalistic moderated by socialist theories and practices or as socialistic moderated by capitalism. The moral principles and consequences of this moderation have formed a significant part of the church's social teaching.

1. Human Rights and Ownership

Private property, including that of productive goods, is a natural right possessed by all, which the state may by no means suppress. However, as there is from nature a social aspect to private property, he who uses his right in this regard must take into account not merely his own welfare but that of others as well. (MM 19)

Ownership and other forms of private control over material goods contribute to the expression of personality. Moreover, they furnish men with an occasion for exercising their role in society and the economy. Hence it is very important to facilitate the access of both individuals and communities to some control over material goods. (GS 71)

Private ownership or some other kind of dominion over material goods provides everyone with a wholly necessary area of independence and should be regarded as an extension of human freedom. Finally since it adds incentives for carrying on one's function and duty, it constitutes a kind of prerequisite for civil liberties. (GS 71)

The forms of such dominion or ownership are varied today and are becoming increasingly diversified. They all remain a source of security not to be underestimated, even in the face of public funds, rights, and services provided by society. This is true not only of material goods but also of intangible goods such as professional skills. (GS 71)

The right of private control, however, is not opposed to the right inherent in various forms of public ownership. Still, goods can be transferred to the public domain only by the competent authority, according to the demands and within the limits of the common good, and with fair compensation. It is a further right of public authority to guard against any misuse of private property which injures the common good. (GS 71)

By its very nature, private property has a social quality deriving from the law of the communal purpose of earthly goods. If this social quality is overlooked, property often becomes an occasion of greed and of serious disturbances. Thus, to those who attack the concept of private property, a pretext is given for calling the right itself into question. (GS 71)

2. Dangers in Socialism and Capitalism

Socialism considers the individual person simply as an element, a molecule within the social organism, so that the good of the individual is completely subordinated to the functioning of the socio-economic mechanism. Socialism likewise maintains that the good of the individual can be realized without reference to free choice. Man is thus reduced to a series of social relationships, and the concept of the person as an autonomous subject of moral decision disappears, the very subject whose decisions build the social order. From this mistaken conception of the person there also arise both the distortion of law, which defines the sphere of the exercise of freedom, and an opposition to private property. A person who is deprived of something he can call his own and of the possibility of earning a living through his own initiative comes to depend on the social machine and on those who control it. This makes it much more difficult for him to recognize his dignity as a person and hinders progress toward the building up of an authentic human community. (CA 13)

The position of "rigid" capitalism continues to remain unacceptable, namely the position that defends the exclusive right to private ownership of the means of production as an untouchable "dogma" of economic life. The principle of respect for work demands that this right should undergo a constructive revision in both theory and in practice. If it is true that capital, as the whole of the means of production, is at the same time the product of the work of generations, it is equally true that capital is being unceasingly created through the work being done with the help of all these means of production, and these means can be seen as a great workbench at which the present generation of workers is working day after day. Obviously we are dealing here with different kinds of work, not only so-called manual labor, but also the many forms of intellectual work, including white-collar work and management. (LE 14)

Therefore, while the position of "rigid" capitalism must undergo continual revision in order to be reformed from the point of view of human rights, both human rights in the widest sense and those linked with man's work, it must be stated that from the same point of view these many deeply desired reforms cannot be achieved by any prior elimination of private ownership of the means of production. For it must be noted that merely taking these means of production (capital) out of the hands of their private owners is not enough to ensure their satisfactory socialization. They cease to be the property of a certain social group, namely the private owners, and become the property of organized society, coming under the administrator and direct control of another group of people, namely those who, though not owning them, from the fact of exercising power in society manage them on the level of the whole national or local economy. (LE 14)

C. Economy, International Cooperation

The modern interconnection between men demands the establishment of greater international cooperation in the economic field. For although nearly all peoples have gained their independence, it is still far from true that they are free from excessive inequalities and from every form of undue dependence or that they have put behind them danger of serious internal difficulties. (GS 85)

The development of any nation depends on human and financial assistance. Through education and professional formation, the citizens of each nation should be prepared to shoulder the various offices of economic and social life. Such preparation needs the help of foreign experts. When they render assistance, these experts should do so not in a lordly fashion but as helpers and co-workers. (GS 85)

The developing nations will be unable to procure the necessary material assistance unless the practices of the modern business world undergo a profound change. Additional help should be offered by advanced nations in the form of either grants or investments. These offers should be made generously and without avarice. They should be accepted honorably. (GS 85)

If an economic order is to be created which is genuine and universal, there must be an abolition of excessive desire for profit, nationalistic pretensions, the lust for political domination, militaristic thinking, and intrigues designed to spread and impose ideologies. (GS 85)

The motivating concern for the poor—who are, in a very meaningful term, "the Lord's poor"—must be translated at all levels into concrete actions until it decisively attains a series of necessary reforms. Each local situation will show what reforms are most urgent and how they can be achieved. But those demanded by the situation of international imbalance must not be forgotten. (SRS 43)

In this respect, I wish to mention specifically: the reform of the international trade system, which is mortgaged to protectionism and increasing bilateralism; the reform of the world monetary and financial system, today recognized as inadequate; the question of technological exchanges and their proper use; the need for a review of the structure of existing international organizations in the framework of an international juridical order. (SRS 43)

The international trade system today frequently discriminates against the products of young industries of the developing countries and discourages the producers of raw materials. There exists, too, a kind of international division of labor, whereby the low cost products of certain countries which lack effective labor laws or which are too weak to apply them are sold in other parts of the world at a considerable profit for the companies engaged in this form of production, which knows no frontiers. (SRS 43)

None of what has been said can be achieved without the collaboration of all—especially the international community—in the framework of a solidarity which includes everyone, beginning with the most neglected. But the developing nations themselves have a duty to practice solidarity among themselves and with the neediest countries of the world. (SRS 45)

Under the current uncertainties, in a society capable of mobilizing immense means but whose cultural and moral reflection is still inadequate with regard to their use in achieving the appropriate ends, we are invited to not give in and to build above all a meaningful future for the generations to come. We should not be afraid to propose new ideas, even if they might destabilize pre-existing balances of power that prevail over the weakest. They are a seed thrown to the ground that will sprout and hurry toward bearing fruit. (*Towards Reforming the International Financial and Monetary Systems in the Context of Global Public Authority*, TR Conclusions)

As Benedict XVI exhorts us, agents on all levels—social, political, economic, professional—are urgently needed who have the courage to serve and to promote the common good through an upright life. Only they will succeed in living and seeing beyond the appearances of things and perceiving the gap between existing reality and untried possibilities. (TR Conclusions)

Paul VI emphasized the revolutionary power of "forward-looking imagination" that can perceive the possibilities inscribed in the present and guide people towards a new future. By freeing his imagination, man frees his existence. Through an effort of community imagination, it is possible to transform not only institutions but also lifestyles and encourage a better future for all peoples. (TR Conclusions)

Modern states became structured wholes over time and reinforced sovereignty within their own territory. But social, cultural, and political conditions have gradually changed. Their interdependence has grown—so it has become natural to think of an international community that is integrated and increasingly ruled by a shared system—but a worse form of nationalism has lingered on, according to which the state feels it can achieve the good of its own citizens in a self-sufficient way. (TR Conclusions)

Today all of this seems anachronistic and surreal, and all the nations, great or small, together with their governments, are called to go beyond the "state of nature" which would keep states in a never-ending struggle with one another. Globalization, despite some of its negative aspects, is unifying peoples more and prompting them to move towards a new "rule of law" on the supranational level, supported by a more intense and fruitful collaboration. With dynamics similar to those that put an end in the past to the "anarchical" struggle between rival clans and kingdoms with regard to the creation of national states, today humanity needs to be committed to the transition from the situation of archaic struggles between national entities to a new model of a more cohesive polyarchic international society that respects every people's identity within the multifaceted riches of a single humanity. (TR Conclusions)

Such a passage, which is already timidly under way, would ensure the citizens of all countries—regardless of their size and power—peace and security; development; and free, stable, and transparent markets. As John Paul II warns us, "Just as the time has finally come when in individual States a system of private vendetta and reprisal has given way to the rule of law, so too a similar step forward is now urgently needed in the international community." (TR Conclusions)

Time has come to conceive of institutions with universal competence, now that vital goods shared by the entire human family are at stake, goods which the individual states cannot promote and protect by themselves. (TR Conclusions)

So conditions exist for definitively going beyond a "Westphalian" international order in which the states feel the need for cooperation but do not seize the opportunity to integrate their respective sovereignties for the common good of peoples. (TR Conclusions)

It is the task of today's generation to recognize and consciously to accept these new world dynamics for the achievement of a universal common good. Of course, this transformation will be made at the cost of a gradual, balanced transfer of a part of each nation's powers to a world authority and to regional authorities, but this is necessary at a time when the dynamism of human society and the economy and the progress of technology are transcending borders, which are in fact already very eroded in a globalized world. (TR Conclusions)

The birth of a new society and the building of new institutions with a universal vocation and competence are a prerogative and a duty for everyone, with no distinction. What is at stake is the common good of humanity and the future itself. (TR Conclusions)

In this context, for every Christian there is a special call of the Spirit to become committed decisively and generously so that the many dynamics under way will be channeled towards prospects of fraternity and the common good. An immense amount of work is to be done towards the integral development of peoples and of every person. As the fathers said at the Second Vatican Council, this is a mission that is both social and spiritual, which "to the extent that the former can contribute to the better ordering

of human society, it is of vital concern to the Kingdom of God."
(TR Conclusions)

D. Environment, Ecology, Consumerism

In our day, there is a growing awareness that world peace is threatened not only by the arms race, regional conflicts, and continued injustices among peoples and nations, but also by a lack of *due respect for nature*, by the plundering of natural resources and by a progressive decline in the quality of life. The sense of precariousness and insecurity that such a situation engenders is a seedbed for collective selfishness, disregard for others, and dishonesty. (*Ecological Crisis*, EC 1)

Faced with widespread destruction of the environment, people everywhere are coming to understand that we cannot continue to use the goods of the earth as we have in the past. The public in general as well as political leaders are concerned about this problem, and experts from a wide range of disciplines are studying its causes. Moreover, a new *ecological awareness* is beginning to emerge which, rather than being downplayed, ought to be encouraged to develop into concrete programs and initiatives. (EC 1)

While the horizon of man is being modified according to the images that are being chosen for him, another transformation is making itself felt, one which is the dramatic and unexpected consequence of human activity. Man is suddenly becoming aware that by an ill-considered exploitation he risks destroying it and becoming in his turn the victim of this degradation. Not only is the material environment becoming a permanent menace—pollution and refuse, new illnesses, and absolute destructive capacity—but the human framework is no longer under man's control, thus creating an environment for tomorrow which may well be intolerable. This is a wide-ranging social problem which concerns the entire human family. (OA 21)

A first consideration is the appropriateness of acquiring a growing awareness of the fact that one cannot use with impunity the different categories of beings, whether living or inanimate—animals, plants, the natural elements—simply as one wishes, according to one's own economic needs. On the contrary, one must take into account the nature of each being and its mutual connection in an ordered system, which is precisely the cosmos. (SRS 34)

A second consideration is based on the realization—which is perhaps more urgent—that natural resources are limited; some are not, as it is said, renewable. Using them as if they were inexhaustible, with absolute dominion, seriously endangers their availability not only for the present generation but above all for generations to come. (SRS 34)

The third consideration refers directly to the consequences on a certain type of development on the quality of life in the industrialized zones. We all know that the direct or indirect result of industrialization is, ever more frequently, the pollution of the environment, with serious consequences for the health of the population. (SRS 34)

Once again, it is evident that development and the planning which governs it and the way in which resources are used must include respect for moral demands. One of the latter undoubtedly imposes limits on the use of the natural world. The dominion granted to man by the Creator is not an absolute power, nor can one speak of a freedom to "use or misuse," or to dispose of things as one pleases. The limitation imposed from the beginning by the Creator himself and expressed symbolically by the prohibition not to "eat of the fruit of the tree" (Gen 2:16–17) shows clearly enough that, when it comes to the natural world, we are subject not only to biological laws but also to moral ones, which cannot be violated with impunity. (SRS 34)

An education in ecological responsibility is urgent: responsibility for oneself, for others, and for the earth. This education cannot be rooted in mere sentiment or empty wishes. Its purposes cannot be ideological or political. It must not be based on a rejection of the modern world or a vague desire to return to some "paradise lost." Instead, a true education in responsibility enlists a genuine conversion in ways of thought and behavior. Churches and religious bodies, non-governmental and governmental organizations, indeed all members of society, have a precise role to play in such education. The first educator, however, is the family, where the child learns to respect his neighbor and to love nature. (EC 13)

Equally worrying is the ecological question which accompanies the problem of consumerism and which is closely connected to it. In his desire to have and to enjoy rather than to be and grow, man consumes the resources of the earth and his own life in an excessive and disordered way. At the root of the senseless destruction of the natural environment lies an anthropological error, which unfortunately is widespread in our day. Man, who discovers his capacity to transform and in a certain sense to create the world through his own work, forgets that this is always based on God's prior and original gift of the things that are. Man thinks he can make arbitrary use of the earth, subjecting it without restraint to his will, as though it did not have its own requisites and a prior God-given purpose, which man can indeed develop but must not betray. Instead of carrying out his role as a cooperator with God in the work of creation, man sets himself up in place of God and thus ends up provoking a rebellion on the part of nature, which is more tyrannized than governed by him. (CA 37)

This may mean making important changes in established lifestyles, in order to limit the waste of environmental and human resources, thus enabling every individual, and all the peoples of the earth to have a sufficient share of those resources. In addition, the new material and spiritual resources must be utilized which are a result of the work and culture of peoples who today are on the margins of the international community, so as to obtain an overall human enrichment of the family of nations. (CA 52)

5
Labor

THE WORKING PERSON, HIS rights and welfare, and the crucial role labor has played in all societies worldwide have been prominently intermixed with the social teaching of the church. This was the principal theme of Leo XIII's encyclical *Rerum Novarum*. Following a continuous development of the moral thinking of the church on this topic, John Paul II has especially probed deeply into the philosophy and spirituality of labor.

A. Work Basic to Life, Dignity

1. Labor the Center of Economic Life

Human labor which is expended in the production and exchange of goods or in the performance of economic services is superior to the other elements of economic life. For the latter have only the nature of tools. (GS 67)

    Whether it is engaged in independently or is paid for by someone else, this labor comes immediately from the person. In a sense, the person stamps the things of nature with his seal and subdues them to his will. It is ordinarily by his labor that a man supports himself and his family, is joined to his fellow men and serves them, and is enabled to exercise genuine charity and be a partner in the work of bringing God's creation to perfection. Indeed, we hold that by offering his labor to God a man becomes associated with the redemptive work itself of Jesus Christ, who conferred an eminent dignity on labor when at Nazareth he worked with his own hands. (GS 67)

2. Purpose of Work

Through work, man must earn his daily bread and contribute to the continual advance of science and technology and, above all, elevating unceasingly the cultural and moral level of the society within which he lives in community with those who belong to the same family. And work means any activity by man, whether manual or intellectual, whatever its nature or circumstances, it means any human activity that can and must be recognized as work, in the midst of all the many activities of which man is capable and to which he is predisposed by his very nature, by virtue of humanity itself. Man is made to be the visible universe and image and likeness of God himself, and he is placed in it in order to subdue the earth. From the beginning, therefore, he is called to work. Work is one of the characteristics that distinguishes man from the rest of creation, whose activities for sustaining their lives cannot be called work. Only man is capable of work, and only man works, at the same time by work occupying his existence on earth. Thus, work bears a particular mark of man and of humanity, the mark of a person operating within a community of persons. And this mark decides its interior characteristics: in a sense it constitutes its very nature. (LE Introduction)

"Man is the primary and fundamental way for the Church" (RH 14) precisely because of the inscrutable mystery of redemption in Christ; and so it is necessary to return constantly to this way and to follow it ever anew in the various aspects in which it shows us all the wealth and at the same time all the toil of human existence on earth. (LE 1)

Work is one of those aspects, a perennial and fundamental one that is always relevant and constantly demands renewed attention and decisive witness. Because fresh questions and problems are always arising, there are always fresh hopes, but also fresh fears and threats connected with this basic dimension of human existence: man's life is built every day from work; from work it derives its specific dignity, but at the same time, work contains the unceasing measure of human toil and suffering and also of the harm and injustice which penetrate deeply into social life within individual nations and on the international level. While it is true that man eats the bread produced by the work of his hands—and this means not only the daily bread by which his body keeps alive but also the bread of science and progress, civilization and culture—it is also a perennial truth that he eats this bread by "the sweat of his face," that is to say, not only by personal effort and toil but also in the midst of many tensions, conflicts, and crises, which in relationship with the reality of work disturb the life of individual societies and also of all humanity. (LE 1)

3. Man as the Subject of Work

In order to continue our analysis of work, an analysis linked with the word of the Bible telling man that he is to subdue the earth, we must concentrate our attention on work in the subjective sense, much more than we did on the objective significance, barely touching on the vast range of problems known intimately and to scholars in various fields and also, according to their specialization, to those who work. If the words of the book of Genesis to which we refer in this analysis of ours speak of work in the objective sense, in an indirect way they also speak only indirectly of the subject of work; but what they say is very eloquent and is full of great significance. (LE 6)

Man has to subdue the earth and dominate it because as the "image of God" he is a person, that is to say, a subjective being capable of acting in a planned and rational way, capable of deciding about himself and with a tendency to self-realization. As a person, man is therefore the subject of work. As a person he works; he performs various actions belonging to the work process; independently of their objective content, these actions must all serve to realize his humanity, to fulfill the calling to be a person that is his by reason of his very humanity. (LE 6)

In the modern period, from the beginning of the industrial age, the Christian truth about work had to oppose the various trends of materialistic and economistic thought, for certain supporters of such ideas, work was understood and treated as a sort of "merchandise" that the worker—especially the industrial worker—sells to the employer, who at the same time is the possessor of the capital, that is to say, all of the working tools and means that make production possible. This way of looking at work was widespread especially in the first half of the nineteenth century. Since then, explicit expressions of this sort have almost disappeared and give way to more human ways of thinking about work and evaluating it. The interaction between the worker and the tools and the means of production has given rise to the development of various forms of capitalism—parallel with various forms of collectivism—into which other socioeconomic elements have entered as a consequence of new concrete circumstances and of the emergence of large transnational enterprises. Nevertheless, the danger of treating work as a special kind of "merchandise" or as an impersonal "force" needed for production (the expression "work force" is in fact in common use) always exists, especially when the whole way of looking at the question of economics is marked by the premises of materialistic economism. (LE 7)

The relationship between labor and capital often shows traits of antagonism that take on new forms with the changing of social and economic contexts. In the past, the origin of conflict between labor and capital was found above all "in the fact that the workers put their powers at the disposal of the entrepreneurs, and those, following the principle of maximum profit, tried to establish the lowest possible wage for the work done by the employees" (LE

11). In our present day, this conflict shows aspects that are new and perhaps more disquieting: scientific and technological progress and the globalization of markets, of themselves a source of development and progress, expose workers to the risk of being exploited by the mechanisms of the economy and the unrestrained quest for productivity. (VS 80)

And yet in spite of all this toil—perhaps, in a sense, because of it—work is a good thing for man. Even though it bears the mark of a "bonum arduum," in the terminology of St. Thomas, this does not take away the fact that, as such, it is a good thing for man. It is not only good in the sense that it is useful or something to enjoy; it is also good as being something worthy, that is to say, something that corresponds to man's dignity, that expresses this dignity and increases it. If one wishes to define more clearly the ethical meaning of work, it is this truth that one must particularly keep in mind. Work is a good thing for man—a good thing for his humanity—because through work man not only transforms nature, adapting it to his own needs but he also achieves fulfillment as a human being and indeed in a sense becomes "more a human being." (LE 9)

4. Spirituality of Work

The Church sees it as her particular duty to form a spirituality of work which will help all people to come closer, through work, to God, the Creator and Redeemer, to participate in his salvific plan for man and the world and to deepen their friendship with Christ in their lives by accepting, through faith, a living participation in his threefold mission as priest, prophet, and king as the Second Vatican Council so eloquently teaches. (LE 24)

Historically, the issue of the just ordering of the collectivity has taken a new dimension with the industrialization of society in the nineteenth century. The rise of modern industry caused the old social order to collapse, while the growth of a class of salaried workers provoked radical changes in the fabric of society. The relationship between capital and labor now became the decisive issue—an issue which in that form was previously unknown. Capital and the means of production were the new source of power which, concentrated in the hands of a few, led to the suppression of the rights of the working class, against which they had to rebel. (*Deus Caritas Est*, DC 26)

B. Labor and Society

Through his labors and native endowments, man has ceaselessly striven to better his life. Today, however, especially with the help of science and technology, he has extended his mastery over nearly the whole of nature and continues to do so. Thanks primarily to increased opportunities for many kinds of interchanges among nations, the human family is gradually recognizing that it comprises a single world community and is making itself so. Hence, many benefits once looked for, especially from heavenly powers, man has now enterprisingly procured for himself. (GS 33)

The mandate to subject to himself the earth and all it contains concerns even the most ordinary everyday activities. For while providing the substance of life for themselves and their families, men and women are performing their activities in a way which appropriately benefits society. They can justly consider that by their labor they are unfolding the Creator's work, consulting the advantages of their brother men, and contributing by their personal industry to the realization in history of the divine plan. (GS 34)

Considering the common good on the national level, the following points are relevant and should not be overlooked: 1) to provide employment for as many workers as possible; 2) to take care lest privileged groups arise even among the workers themselves; 3) to maintain a balance between wages and prices; 4) to make accessible the goods and services for a better life to as many persons as possible; 5) either to eliminate or keep within bounds the inequalities that exist between different sectors of the economy—that is, between agriculture, industry and services; 6) to balance properly any increase in output with advances in services provided to citizens, especially by public authority; 7) to adjust, as far as possible, the means of production to the progress of science and technology; 8) finally, to ensure the advantages of a more humane way of existence not merely subserve the present generation but have regard for future generations as well. (MM 79)

With demographic growth, which is particularly pronounced in the young nations, the number of those failing to find work and driven to misery or parasitism will grow in the coming years unless the conscience of man rouses itself and gives rise to a general movement of solidarity through an effective policy of investment and of organization of production and trade, as well as of education. We know the attention given to these problems within international organizations, and it is our lively wish that their members will not delay bringing their actions into line with their declarations. (OA 18)

C. Organization of Labor

In the first place, employers and workmen may themselves effect much in the matter of which we treat, by means of those institutions and organizations which afford opportune assistance to those in need, and which draw the two orders more closely together. Among these may be enumerated: societies for mutual help; various foundations established by private persons for providing for the workmen and for the widow or his orphans in sudden calamity, in sickness, or in the event of death; and what are called "patronage," or institutions for the care of boys and girls, for young people, and also those of more mature age. (RN 36)

The most important of all are workmen's associations; for these virtually include all the rest. History attests what excellent results were effected by the artificers' guilds of a former day. They were the means not only of many advantages to the workmen but in no small degree of the advancement of art, as numerous monuments remain to prove. Associations should be adapted to the requirements of the age in which we live—an age of great instruction, of different customs, and of more numerous requirements in daily life. It is gratifying to know that there are actually in existence not a few societies of this nature, consisting either of workmen alone or of workmen and employers together; but it were greatly to be desired that they should multiply and become more effective. We have spoken of them more than once; but it will be well to explain here how much they are needed to show that they exist by their own right and to enter into their organization and their work. (RN 36)

Worthy of all praise, therefore, are the directions authoritatively promulgated by Leo XIII, which served to break down opposition and dispel suspicions. They have a still higher distinction, however, that of encouraging Christian workmen to form unions according to their several trades and of teaching them how to do it. Many were thus confirmed in the path of duty, in spite of very strong attractions of socialist organizations, which claimed to be the sole defenders and champions of the lowly and the oppressed. (QA 31)

Among the basic rights of the human person must be counted the right of freely founding labor unions. These unions should be truly able to represent the workers and to contribute to the proper arrangement of economic life. Another such right is that of taking part freely in the activities of these unions without risk of reprisal. Through this sort of orderly participation, joined with an ongoing formation in economic and social matters, all will grow day by day in the awareness of their own function and responsibility. Thus, they will be brought to feel that according to their own proper capacities and aptitudes they are associates in the whole task of economic and social development and in the attainment of the universal common good. (GS 68)

All workers' rights, together with the need for the workers themselves to secure them, give rise to yet another right: the right of association, that is, to form associations for the purpose of defending the vital interests of those employed in the various professions. These associations are called labor or trade unions. The vital interests of the worker are to a certain extent common for all of them; at the same time, however, each type of work, each profession, has its own specific character which should find a particular reflection in these organizations. (LE 20)

The important role of union organizations must be admitted: their object is the representation of the various categories of workers, their lawful collaboration in the economic advance of society, and the development of the sense of their responsibility for the realization of the common good. Their activity, however, is not without its difficulties. Here and there the temptation can arise of profiting from a position or force to impose, particularly by strikes—the right to which as a final means of defense remains certainly recognized—conditions which are too burdensome for the overall economy and for the social body, or to desire to obtain in this way demands of a directly political nature. When it is a question of public service, required for the life of the entire nation, it is necessary to be able to assess the limit beyond which the harm caused to society becomes inadmissible. (CA 14)

D. Duties and Rights of Labor

While work, in all its many senses, is an obligation, that is to say a duty, it is also a source of rights on the part of the worker. These rights must be examined in the broad context of human rights as a whole, which are connatural with man and many of which are proclaimed by various international organizations and increasingly guaranteed by the individual states for their citizens. Respect for this broad range of human rights constitutes the fundamental condition for peace in the modern world: peace both within individual countries and societies and in international relations, as the Church's Magisterium has several times noted, especially since the Encyclical *Pacem in Terris*. The human rights which flow from work are part of the broader context of those fundamental rights of the person. (LE 16)

Wherefore, we judge it our duty to reaffirm once again that just as remuneration for work cannot be left entirely to unregulated competition, neither may it be decided arbitrarily at the will of the most powerful. Rather, in this matter, the norms of justice and equity should be strictly observed. This requires that workers receive a wage sufficient to lead a life worthy of man and to fulfill family responsibilities properly. But in determining what constitutes an appropriate wage, the following must necessarily be taken into account: first of all, the contribution of individuals to the economic effort; the economic state of the enterprises within which they work; the requirements of each community, especially as regards overall employment; finally, what concerns the common good of all peoples, namely, of various states associated among themselves but differing in character and extent. (MM 71)

The key problem of social ethics in this case is that of just remuneration for work done. In the context of the present, there is no more important way for securing a just relationship between the worker and the employer than that constituted by remuneration for work. Whether the work is done in a system of private ownership of the means of production or in a system where ownership has undergone a certain "socialization," the relationship between the employer (first and foremost the direct employer) and the worker is resolved on the basis of the wage, that is, through just remuneration of the work done. (LE 19)

From all these considerations there arise every man's duty to labor faithfully and also his right to work. It is the duty of society, moreover, according to the circumstances prevailing in it, and in keeping with its proper role, to help its citizens find opportunities for adequate employment. Finally, payment for labor must be such as to furnish a man with the means to cultivate his own material, social, cultural, and spiritual life worthily, and that of his dependents. What this payment should be will vary according to each man's assignment and productivity, the conditions of his place of employment, and the common good. (GS 67)

Since economic activity is generally exercised through the combined labors of human beings, any way of organizing and directing that activity which would be detrimental to any worker would be wrong and inhuman. It too often happens, however, even in our day, that in one way or another workers are made slaves of their work. This situation can by no means be justified by so-called economic laws. The entire process of productive work, therefore, must be adapted to the needs of the person and to the requirements of his life. Such is especially the case with respect to the mothers of families, but due consideration must be given to every person's sex and age. (GS 67)

The opportunities should also be afforded to workers to develop their own abilities through the work they perform. Though they should apply their time and energy to their employment with a due sense of responsibility, all workers should also enjoy sufficient rest and leisure to cultivate their family, cultural, social, and religious life. They should also have the opportunity to develop on their own the resources and potentialities to which, perhaps, their professional work gives but little scope. (GS 67)

E. Some Labor Problems

If the demands of justice and equity are to be satisfied, vigorous efforts must be made, without violence to the right of persons or to the natural characteristics of each country, to remove as quickly as possible the immense economic inequalities which now exist. In many cases, these are worsening and are connected with individual and group discrimination. (GS 66)

In many areas, too, farmers experience special difficulties in raising products or selling them. In such cases, country people must be helped to increase and to market what they produce, to make the necessary advances and changes, and to obtain a fair return. Otherwise, as too often happens, they will remain in the condition of lower-class citizens. Let farmers, especially young ones, skillfully apply themselves to perfecting their professional competence. Without it, no agricultural progress can take place. (GS 66)

Justice and equity also require that the mobility which is necessary in a developing economy be regulated in such a way as to keep the life of individuals and their families from becoming insecure and precarious. Hence, when workers come from another country or district and contribute by their labor to the economic advancement of a nation or region, all discrimination with respect to wages and working conditions must be carefully avoided. (GS 66)

The local people, moreover, especially public authorities, should all treat them not as mere tools of production but as persons and must help them to arrange for their families to live with them and to provide themselves with decent living quarters. The native should also see that these workers are introduced into the social life of the country or region which receives them. Employment opportunities, however, should be created in their own areas as far as possible. (GS 66)

In those economic affairs which are today subject to change, as in the new forms of industrial society in which automation, for example, is advancing, care must be taken that sufficient and suitable work can be obtained, along with appropriate technical and professional formation. The livelihood and the human dignity of those, especially who are in particularly difficult circumstances because of illness or old age, should be safeguarded. (GS 66)

The fact is that many people, perhaps the majority today, do not have the means which would enable them to take their place in an effective and humanly dignified way within a productive system in which work is truly central. They have no way of acquiring the basic knowledge which would enable them to express their creativity and develop their potential. They have no way of entering the network of knowledge and intercommunication which would enable them to see their qualities appreciated and utilized. Thus, if not actually exploited, they are to a great extent marginalized; economic development takes place over their heads, so to speak, when it does not actually reduce the already narrow scope of their subsistence economies. They are unable to compete against the goods which are produced in ways which are new and which properly respond to needs, needs which they had previously been accustomed to meeting through traditional forms of organization. Allured by the dazzle of an opulence which is beyond their reach, and where they are exposed to situations of violent uncertainty, without the possibility of becoming integrated. Their dignity is not acknowledged in any real way and sometimes there are even attempts to eliminate them from history through coercive forms of demographic control which are contrary to human dignity. (CA 33)

It is wrong to abuse the tender age of children or the weakness of women. Mothers should especially devote their energies to the home and the things connected with it. Most unfortunate, and to be remedied energetically, is the abuse whereby mothers of families, because of the insufficiency of the father's salary, are forced to engage in gainful occupations outside the domestic walls to the neglect of their own proper cares and duties, particularly the education of their children. (QA 71)

Recently, national communities and international organizations have turned their attention to another question connected with work, one full of implications: the question of disabled persons. They too are fully human subjects with corresponding innate, sacred, and inviolable rights, and, in spite of the limitations and sufferings affecting their bodies and faculties, they point up more clearly the dignity and greatness of man. Since disabled people are subjects with all of their rights, they should be helped to participate in the life of society in all of its aspects and at all levels accessible to their capacities. The disabled person is one of us and participates fully in the humanity that we possess. It would be radically unworthy of man, and a denial of our common humanity, to admit to the life of the community, and thus to admit to work, only those who are fully functional. To do so would be to practice a serious form of discrimination, that of the strong and healthy against the weak and sick. Work in the objective sense should be subordinated, in this circumstance too, to the dignity of man, to the subject of work, and not to economic advantage. (LE 22)

The role of the agents included under the title of indirect employer is to act against unemployment, which in all cases is an evil and which, when it reaches a certain level, can become a social disaster. It is particularly painful when it especially affects young people who after appropriate cultural, technical, and professional preparation fail to find work and see their sincere wish to work and their readiness to take on their own responsibility for the economic and social development of the community sadly frustrated. The obligation to provide unemployment benefits, that is to say, the duty to make suitable grants indispensable for the subsistence of unemployed workers and their families, is a duty springing from the fundamental principle of the moral order in this sphere, namely, the principle of the common use of goods or, to put it in another and still simpler way, the right to life and subsistence. (LE 18)

6

Political Community

A. Political Community and Public Authority

1. Public Authority, Common Good, Rights of Citizens

THE CHURCH HAS ALWAYS considered ways of understanding authority, taking care to defend and propose a model of authority that is founded on the social nature of the person. Since God made men social by nature, and since no society can hold together unless someone be over all, directing all to strive earnestly for the common good, every civilized community must have a ruling authority, and this authority, no less than society itself, has its source in nature, and has, consequently, God for its author. Political authority is, therefore, necessary because of the responsibilities assigned to it. Political authority is and must be a positive and irreplaceable component of civil life. (PT 55)

Our times have witnessed profound changes in the institution of peoples and in the ways that people are joined together. These changes are resulting from the cultural, economic, and social evolution of these same peoples. The changes are having a

Political Community

great impact on the life of the political community, especially with regard to universal rights and duties in the exercise of civil liberty and in the attainment of the common good and with regard to the regulation of the relation of citizens among themselves and with public authority. (GS 73)

From a keener awareness of human dignity there arises in many parts of the world a desire to establish a political-juridic order in which personal rights can gain greater protection. These include the rights of free assembly, of common action, of expressing personal opinions, and of professing a religion both privately and publicly. For the protection of personal rights is a necessary condition for the active participation of citizens, whether as individuals or collectively, in the life and government of the state. Men are voicing disapproval of any kind of government which blocks civil or religious liberty, multiplies the victims of ambition and political crimes, and wrenches the authority from pursuing the common good to serving the advantage of a certain faction or of the rulers themselves. There are some such governments holding power in the world. (GS 73)

Individuals, families, and various groups which compose the civic community are aware of their own insufficiency in the matter of establishing a fully human condition of life. They see the need for that wider community in which each would daily contribute his energies toward the even better attainment of the common good. It is for this reason that they set up the political community in its manifold expressions. (GS 74)

Hence the political community exists for that common good in which the community finds its full justification and meaning, and from which it derives its pristine and proper right. Now the common good embraces the sum of those conditions of social life by which individuals, families, and groups can achieve their fulfillment in a relatively thorough and ready way. (GS 74)

Many different people go to make up the political community, and these can lawfully incline toward diverse ways of doing things. Now, if the political community is not to be torn to pieces as each man follows his own viewpoint, authority is needed. This authority must dispose the energies of the whole citizenry toward the common good, not mechanically or despotically, but primarily as a moral force which depends on freedom and the conscientious discharge of the burdens of any office which has been undertaken. (GS 74)

It is therefore obvious that the political community and public authority are based on human nature and hence belong to an order of things divinely foreordained. At the same time, the choice of government and the method of selecting leaders are left to the free will of citizens. (GS 74)

Human society can be neither well-ordered nor prosperous unless it has some people vested with legitimate authority to preserve its institutions and to devote themselves as far as is necessary to work and care for the good of all. These, however, derive their authority from God, as St. Paul teaches in the words: "Authority comes from God alone" (Rom 13:1). Moreover, since God made men social by nature, and since no society "can hold together unless someone be over all, directing all to strive earnestly for the common good, every civilized community must have a ruling authority, no less than society itself, has its source in nature, and has, consequently, God for its author" (Leo XIII, *Immortale Dei*). (PT 46)

It must not be concluded, however, because authority comes from God, therefore men have no right to choose those who are to rule the state, to decide the form of government, and to determine both the way in which authority is to be exercised and its limits. It is thus clear that the doctrine which we have set forth can be fully consonant with any truly democratic regime. (PT 52)

2. Structure of Government

It is impossible to determine in all cases how civil authorities can most effectively fulfill their respective functions, i.e., the legislative, judicial, and executive functions of the state. (PT 67)

It is unquestionable that a legal structure in conformity with the moral order and corresponding to the level of development of the state is of great advantage to achievement of the common good. (PT 70)

From these considerations it becomes clear that in the juridical organization of states in our times the first requisite is that a charter of fundamental human rights be drawn up in clear and precise terms and that it be incorporated in its entirety in the constitution. (PT 75)

If conscientious cooperation between citizens is to achieve its happy effect in the normal course of public affairs, a positive system of law is required. In it should be established a division of governmental roles and institutions and at the same time an effective and independent system for the protection of rights. Let the rights of all persons, families, and associations, along with the exercise of those rights, be recognized, honored, and fostered. The same holds for those duties which bind all citizens. Among the latter should be remembered that of furnishing the commonwealth with the material and spiritual services required for the common good. (GS 75)

Following the collapse of communist totalitarianism and of many other totalitarian and "national security" regimes, today we are witnessing a predominance, not without signs of opposition, of the democratic ideal, together with lively attention to and concern for human rights. But for this very reason it is necessary for peoples in the process of reforming their systems to give democracy an authentic and solid foundation through the explicit recognition of those rights. Among the most important of these rights, mention must be made of the right to life, an integral part of which is the right of the child to develop in the mother's womb from the moment of conception; the right to live in a united family and in a moral environment conducive to the growth of the child's personality; the right to develop one's intelligence and freedom in seeking and knowing the truth; the right to share in the work which makes wise use of the earth's material resources and to derive from that work the means to support oneself and one's dependents; and the right freely to establish a family, to have and to rear children through the responsible exercise of one's sexuality. In a certain sense, the source and synthesis of these rights is religious freedom, understood as the right to live in the truth of one's faith and in conformity with one's transcendent dignity as a person. (CA 47)

In recent years the range of such (social) intervention has vastly expanded, to the point of creating a new type of state, the so-called "welfare state." This has happened in some countries in order to respond better to many needs and demands, by remedying many forms of poverty and deprivation unworthy of the human person. However, excesses and abuses, especially in recent years, have provoked very harsh criticism of the welfare state, dubbed the "social assistance state." Malfunctions and defects in the social assistance state are the result of an inadequate understanding of the tasks proper to the state. Here again, the principle of subsidiarity must be respected: a community of a higher order should not interfere in the internal life of a community of a lower order, depriving the latter of its functions, but rather should support it in the case of need and help to coordinate its activity with the activities of the rest of society, always with a view to the common good. (CA 48)

It must also be restated that no social group, for example a political party, has the right to usurp the role of sole leader, since this brings about the destruction of the true subjectivity of society of the individual citizens, as happens in every form of totalitarianism. In this situation the individual and the people become "objects," in spite of all declarations to the contrary and verbal assurances. (SRS 15)

B. Citizen Participation

It is in full accord with human nature that juridical-political structures should, with ever better success and without any discrimination, afford all of their citizens the chance to participate freely and actively in establishing the constitutional bases of a political community, governing the state, determining the scope and purpose of various institutions, and choosing leaders. Hence let all citizens be mindful of their simultaneous right and duty to vote freely in the interest of advancing the common good. The Church regards as worthy of praise and consideration the work of those who, as a service to others, dedicate themselves to the welfare of the state and undertake the burdens of this task. (GS 75)

Christians should recognize that the various legitimate though conflicting views can be held concerning the regulation of temporal affairs. They should respect their fellow citizens when they promote such views honorably even by group action. Political parties should foster whatever they judge necessary for the common good. But they should never prefer their own advantage over this same common good. (GS 75)

Civic and political education is today supremely necessary for the people, especially young people. Such education should be painstakingly provided so that all citizens can make their contribution to the political community. Let those who are suited for it, or can become so, prepare themselves for the difficult but most honorable art of politics. Let them work to exercise this art without thought of personal convenience and without benefit of bribery. Prudently and honorably let them fight against injustice and oppression, the arbitrary rule of one man or one party, and lack of tolerance. Let them devote themselves to the welfare of all sincerely and fairly, indeed with charity and political courage. (GS 75)

The Church values the democratic system inasmuch as it ensures the participation of citizens in making political choices, guarantees to the governed the possibility of both electing and holding accountable those who govern them and of replacing them through peaceful means when appropriate. Thus, she cannot encourage the formation of narrow ruling groups which usurp the power of the state for individual interests or for ideological ends. (CA 46)

C. Political Community and the Church

It is highly important, especially in pluralistic societies, that a proper view exist of the relation between the political community and the Church. Thus the faithful will be able to make a clear distinction between what a Christian conscience leads them to do in their own name as citizens, whether as individuals or in association, and what they do in the name of the Church and in union with her shepherds. (GS 76)

The role and competence of the Church being what it is, she must in no way be confused with the political community nor bound to any political system. For she is at once a sign and a safeguard of the transcendence of the human person. (GS 76)

In their proper sphere, the political community and the Church are mutually independent and self-governing. Yet, by a different title, each serves the personal and social vocation of the same human beings. This service can be more effectively rendered for the good of all if each works better for wholesome mutual cooperation, depending on the circumstances of time and place. For man is not restricted to the temporal sphere. While living in history, he fully maintains his eternal vocation. (GS 76)

The Church, founded on the Redeemer's love, contributes to the wider application of justice and charity within and between nations. By preaching the truth of the Gospel and shedding light on all areas of human activity through her teaching and the example of the faithful, she shows respect for the political freedom and responsibility of citizens and fosters these values. (GS 76)

The present situation of the world demands concerted action based on a clear vision of all economic, social, and spiritual aspects. Experienced in human affairs, the Church, without attempting to interfere in any way in the politics of states, "seeks but a solitary goal: to carry forward the work of Christ himself under the lead of the befriending Spirit. And Christ entered this world to give witness to the truth, to rescue and not sit in judgment, to serve and not to be served" (GS 63). Founded to establish on earth the kingdom of heaven and not to conquer any earthly power, the Church clearly states that the two realms are distinct, just as the two powers, ecclesiastical and civil, are supreme, each in its own domain. But since the Church lives in history, she ought to "scrutinize the signs of the times and interpret them in the light of the Gospel" (GS 4). Sharing the noblest aspirations of man and suffering when she sees them not satisfied, she wishes to help them attain their full flowering, and that is why she offers men what she possesses as the characteristic attribute: a global vision of man and of the human race. (PP 13)

D. Peace

1. Meaning of Peace

Peace on earth, which all men of every era have most eagerly longed for, can be firmly established only if the order laid down by God be dutifully observed. (PT 1)

In our generation when men continue to be afflicted by acute hardships and anxieties arising from ongoing wars or the threat of them, the whole human family has reached an hour of supreme crisis in its advance toward maturity. Moving gradually together and everywhere more conscious already of its oneness, this family cannot accomplish its task of constructing for all men everywhere a world more genuinely human unless each person devotes himself with renewed determination to the reality of peace. Thus it happens that the gospel message, which is in harmony with the loftier strivings and aspirations of the human race, takes on a new luster in our days as it declares that the artisans of peace are blessed, "for they shall be called children of God" (Matt 5:9). (GS 77)

Consequently, as it points out the authentic and most noble meaning of peace and condemns the frightfulness of war, the council fervently desires to summon Christians to cooperate with all men in making secure among themselves a peace based on justice and love and in setting up agencies of peace. This Christians should do with the help of Christ, the Author of Peace. (GS 77)

Peace is not merely the absence of war. Nor can it be reduced solely to the maintenance of a balance of power between enemies. Nor is it brought about by dictatorship. Instead, it is rightly and appropriately called "an enterprise of justice" (Isa 32:7). Peace results from that harmony built into human society by its divine

Founder and actualized by men as they thirst after ever-greater justice. (GS 78)

The common good of men is in its basic sense determined by the eternal law. Still, the concrete demands of this common good are constantly changing as time goes on. Hence peace is never attained once and for all but must be built up ceaselessly. Moreover, since the human will is unsteady and wounded by sin, the achievement of peace requires that everyone constantly master his passions and that lawful authority keep vigilant. (GS 78)

But such is not enough. This peace cannot be attained on earth unless personal values are safeguarded and men freely and trustingly share with one another the riches of their inner spirits and their talents. A firm determination to respect other men and peoples and their dignity, as well as the studied practice of brotherhood, are absolutely necessary for the establishment of peace. Hence, peace is likewise the fruit of love, which goes beyond what justice can provide. (GS 78)

2. Avoidance of War

In spite of the fact that recent wars have wrought physical and moral havoc on our world, conflicts still produce their devastating effect day by day somewhere in the world. Indeed, now that every kind of weapon produced by modern science is used in war, the fierce character of warfare threatens to lead the combatants to a savagery far surpassing that of the past. Furthermore, the complexity of the modern world and the intricacy of international relations allow guerrilla warfare to be drawn out by new methods of deceit and subversion. In many cases the use of terrorism is regarded as a new way to wage war. (GS 79)

Contemplating this melancholy state of humanity, the Council wishes to recall first of all the permanent binding force of natural law and its all-embracing principles. Man's conscience itself gives ever more emphatic voice to these principles. Therefore, actions which deliberately conflict with these same principles, as well as orders commanding such actions, are criminal. Blind obedience cannot excuse those who yield to them. Among such must first be counted those actions designed for the methodical extermination of an entire people, nation, or ethnic minority. These actions must be vehemently condemned as horrendous crimes. The courage of those who openly and fearlessly resist men who issue such commands merits supreme commendation. (GS 79)

On the subject of war, quite a number of nations have subscribed to various international agreements aimed at making military activity and its consequences less inhuman. Such are the conventions concerning the handling of wounded or captured soldiers and various similar agreements. Agreements of this sort must be honored. Indeed they should be improved upon so that they can better and more workably lead to restraining the frightfulness of war. (GS 79)

All men, especially government officials and experts in these matters, are bound to do everything they can to effect these improvements. Moreover, it seems right that laws make humane provisions for the cases of those who for reason of conscience refuse to bear arms provided, however, that they accept some other form of service to the human community. (GS 79)

3. Disarmament

It is with deep sorrow that we note the enormous stocks of armaments that have been and still are being made in more economically developed countries, with a vast outlay of intellectual and economic resources. And so it happens that, while people of these countries are loaded with heavy burdens, other countries as a result are deprived of the collaboration they need in order to make economic and social progress. (PT 109)

The production of arms is allegedly justified on the grounds that in present-day conditions peace cannot be preserved without an equal balance of armaments. And so if one country increases its armaments, others feel the need to do the same; and if one country is equipped with nuclear weapons, other countries must produce their own, equally destructive. (PT 110)

Consequently, people live in constant fear lest the storm that every moment threatens should break upon them with dreadful violence. And with good reason, for the arms of war are ready at hand. Even though it is difficult to believe that anyone would dare bring upon himself the appalling destruction and sorrow that war would bring in its train, it cannot be denied that the conflagration can be set off by some unexpected and unpremeditated act. And one must bear in mind that, even though the monstrous power of modern weapons act as a deterrent, there is nevertheless reason to fear that the mere continuance of nuclear tests, undertaken with war in mind, can seriously jeopardize various kinds of life on earth. (PT 111)

Justice, then right reason, and consideration for human dignity and life, urgently demand that the arms race should cease, that the stockpiles which exist in various countries should be reduced equally and simultaneously by the parties concerned, that nuclear weapons should be banned, and finally that all come to an agreement on a fitting program of disarmament, employing mutual and effective controls. In the words of Pius XII, our predecessor of happy memory: "The calamity of a world war, with the economic and social ruin and the moral excesses and dissolution that accompany it, must not be permitted to envelop the human race for a third time" (Radio Message, December 24, 1941). (PT 112)

All must realize that there is no hope of putting an end to the building up of armaments nor of reducing the present stock nor, still less, (and this is the main point) of abolishing them altogether, unless the process is complete and thorough and unless it proceeds from inner conviction: unless, that is, everyone sincerely cooperates to banish the fear and anxious expectation of war with which men are oppressed. If this is to come about, the fundamental principle on which our present peace depends must be replaced by another, which declares that the true and solid peace of nations consists not in equality of arms but in mutual trust alone. We believe that this can be brought to pass, and we consider that, since it concerns a matter not only demanded by right reason but also eminently desirable in itself, it will prove to be the source of many benefits. (PT 113)

In the first place, it is an objective demanded by reason. There can be, or at least should be, no doubt that relations between states, as between individuals, should be regulated not by force of arms but by the light of reason, by the rule, that is, of truth, of justice, and of active and sincere cooperation. (PT 114)

Secondly, we say that it is an objective earnestly to be desired in itself. Is there anyone who does not ardently yearn to see dangers of war abolished, to see peace preserved and daily more firmly established? (PT 115)

And, finally, it is an objective which will be a fruitful source of many benefits for its advantages will be felt everywhere, by individuals, by families, by nations, by the whole human family. The warning of Pius XII still rings in our ears: "Nothing is lost by peace; everything may be lost by war" (Radio Message, August 24, 1939). (PT 116)

The horror and perversity of war are immensely magnified by the multiplication of scientific weapons. For acts of war involving these weapons can inflict massive and indiscriminate destruction far exceeding the bounds of legitimate defense. Indeed, if the kind of instruments which can now be found in the armories of the great nations were to be employed to their fullest, an almost total and altogether reciprocal slaughter of each side by the other would follow, not to mention the widespread devastation which would take place in the world and the deadly aftereffects which would be spawned by the use of such weapons. (GS 80)

All these considerations compel us to undertake an evaluation of war with an entirely new attitude. The men of our time must realize that they will have to give a somber reckoning for their deeds of war. For the course of the future will depend largely on the decisions they make today. (GS 80)

Scientific weapons, to be sure, are not amassed solely for use in war. The defensive strength of any nation is considered to be dependent upon its capacity for immediate retaliation against an adversary. Hence this accumulation of arms, which increases each year, also serves, in a way heretofore unknown, as a deterrent to possible enemy attack. Many regard this state of affairs as the most effective way by which peace of a sort can be maintained between nations at the present time. (GS 81)

Warned by the calamities which the human race has made possible, let us make use of the interlude granted us from above and in which we rejoice. In greater awareness of our own responsibility, let us find means for resolving our disputes in a manner more worthy of man. Divine providence urgently demands of us that we free ourselves from the age-old slavery of war. But if we refuse to make this effort, we do not know where the evil road we have ventured upon will lead us. (GS 81)

E. International Political Community

1. Need for World Governance

Since the relationships between countries today are closer in every region of the world, by reason of science and technology, it is proper that peoples become more and more interdependent. (MM 200)

Accordingly, contemporary problems of moment—whether in the fields of science and technology or of economic and social affairs or of public administration or of cultural advancement—these, because they may exceed the capacities of individual states, very often affect a number of nations and at times all the nations of the earth. (MM 201)

As a result, individual countries, although advanced in culture and civilization, in number and industry of citizens, in wealth, in geographical extent, are not able by themselves to resolve satisfactorily their basic problems. Accordingly, because states must on occasion complement or perfect one another, they really consult their own interests only when they take into account at the same time the interest of others. Hence, dire necessity warns commonwealths to cooperate among themselves and provide mutual assistance. (MM 202)

2. Solidarity and Interdependence

Since the mutual relations among nations must be regulated by the norm of truth and justice, they must also derive great advantage from a union of mind, heart, and resources. This can be effected at various levels by mutual cooperation in many ways, as is happening in our own time with beneficial results in the economic, social, politic, educational, public health, and sports spheres. We must remember that, of its very nature, civil authority exists not to confine its people within the boundaries of their nation but rather to protect, above all else, the common good of the entire human family. (PT 98)

So it happens that civil societies in pursuing their interests not only must not harm others but must join their plans and forces whenever the efforts of an individual government cannot achieve its desired goals; but in the execution of such common efforts, great care must be taken lest what helps some nations should injure others. (PT 99)

The recent progress of science and technology, since it has profoundly influenced human conduct, is rousing men everywhere in the world to more and more cooperation and association with one another. Today the exchange of goods and ideas as well as travel from one country to another have greatly increased. Consequently, the close relations of individuals, families, intermediate associations belonging to different countries have become vastly more frequent and conferences between heads of state are held at shorter intervals. At the same time, the interdependence of national economies has grown deeper, one becoming more closely related to the other, so that they become, as it were, integral parts of the one world economy. Finally, the social progress, order, security, and peace of each country are necessarily connected with the social progress, order, security, and peace of all other countries. (PT 130)

Given these conditions, it is obvious that individual countries cannot rightly seek their own interests and develop themselves in isolation from the rest, for the prosperity and development of one country follows partly in the train of the prosperity and progress of all the rest and partly produces that prosperity and progress. (PT 131)

Just as it is necessary in each state that relations which the public authority has with its citizens, families, and intermediate associations be controlled and regulated by the principle of subsidiarity, it is equally necessary that the relationship which exists between the worldwide public authority and the public authorities of individual nations be governed by the same principle. This means that the worldwide public authority must tackle and solve problems of an economic, social, political, or cultural character which are posed by the universal common good. For, because of the vastness, complexity, and urgency of those problems, the public authorities of the individual states are not in a position to tackle them with any hope of a positive solution. (PT 140)

F. Liberation Theology

1. Liberation and Evangelization

Evangelization would not be complete if it did not take account of the unceasing interplay of the Gospel and man's concrete life, both personal and social. This is why evangelization involves an explicit message, adapted to the different situations constantly being realized, about the rights and duties of every human being, about family life without which personal growth and development is hardly possible, about life in society, about international life, peace, justice, and development—a message especially energetic today about liberation. (*Evangelii Nuntiandi*, EN 29)

It is well known in what terms numerous bishops from all the continents spoke of this at the last Synod, especially the bishops from the Third World, with a pastoral accent resonant with the voice of the millions of sons and daughters of the Church in these nations. Peoples, as we know, engaged with all of their energy in the effort and struggle to overcome everything which condemns them to remain on the margin of life: famine, chronic

Political Community

disease, illiteracy, poverty, injustice in international relations and especially in commercial exchanges, situations of economic and cultural neo-colonialism sometimes as cruel as the old political colonialism. The church, as the bishops repeated, has the duty to proclaim the liberation of millions of human beings, many of whom are her own children—the duty of assisting the birth of this liberation, of giving witness to it, of assuring that it is complete. This is not foreign to evangelization. (EN 30)

Between evangelization and human advancement—development and liberation—there are in fact profound links. These include links of an anthropological order, because the man who is to be evangelized is not an abstract being but is subject to social and economic questions. They also include links in the theological order, since one cannot dissociate the plan of creation from the plan of Redemption. The latter touches the very concrete situation of injustice to be combatted and the justice to be restored. They include links of the eminently evangelical order, which is that of charity: how in fact can one proclaim the new commandment without promoting in justice and in peace the true, authentic advancement of man? We ourselves have taken care to point this out, by recalling that it is impossible to accept that in evangelization one could or should ignore the importance of the problem so much discussed today concerning justice, liberation, development, and peace in the world. This would be to forget the lesson which comes to us from the Gospel concerning love of our neighbor who is suffering and in need. (EN 31)

2. Theological Meaning of Liberation

We must not ignore the fact that many, even generous Christians who are sensitive to the dramatic questions involved in the problem of liberation, in their wish to commit the Church to the liberation effort are frequently tempted to reduce her mission to the dimensions of a simply temporal project. They would reduce her aims to a man-centered goal; the salvation of which she is the messenger would be reduced to material well-being. Her activity, forgetful of all spiritual and religious preoccupation, would become initiatives of the political and social order. But if this were so, the Church would lose her fundamental meaning. Her message of liberation would no longer have any originality and would easily be open to monopolization and manipulation by ideological systems and political parties. She would have no more authority to proclaim freedom in the name of God. That is why we have wished to emphasize, in the same address at the opening of the Synod, the need to restate clearly the specifically religious finality of evangelization. This latter would lose its reason for existence if it were to diverge from the religious axis that guides it; the Kingdom of God, before anything else, is its fully theological meaning. (EN 32)

With regard to the liberation which evangelization proclaims and strives to put into practice one should rather say this: 1) it cannot be contained in the simple and restrictive dimension of economics, politics, social, or cultural life; it must envision the whole man, in all his aspects, right up to and including his openness to the absolute, even the divine Absolute; 2) it is therefore attached to a certain concept of man, to a view of man which it can never sacrifice to the needs of any strategy, practice, or short-term efficiency. (EN 33)

Hence, when preaching liberation and associating herself with those who are working and suffering for it, the Church is certainly not willing to restrict her mission only to the religious field and dissociate herself from man's temporal problems. Nevertheless, she reaffirms the primacy of her spiritual vocation and refuses to replace the proclamation of the kingdom by the proclamation of forms of human liberation; she even states that her contribution to liberation is incomplete if she neglects to proclaim salvation in Jesus Christ. (EN 34)

The Church links liberation and salvation in Jesus Christ, but she never identifies them because she knows through revelation, historical experience, and the reflection of faith that not every notion of liberation is necessarily consistent and compatible with an evangelical vision of man, of things and events; she knows too that in order that God's kingdom should come it is not enough to establish liberation and create well-being and development. (EN 35)

And what is more, the Church has the firm conviction that all temporal liberation—even if it endeavors to find its justification in such or such page of the Old or New Testament, even if it claims for its ideological postulates development which is merely economic—is incapable of setting man free; on the contrary, it will end by enslaving him further. Development which does not include the cultural, transcendent, and religious dimensions of man and society, to the extent that it does not recognize the existence of such dimensions and does not endeavor to direct its goals and priorities toward the same, is even less conducive to authentic liberation. Human beings are totally free only when they are completely "themselves," in the fullness of their rights and duties. The same can be said about society as a whole. (SRS 46)

The principal obstacle to be overcome on the way to authentic liberation is sin and the structures produced by sin as it multiplies and spreads. (SRS 46)

Thus, the process of liberation and development takes concrete shape in the exercise of solidarity, that is to say in the love and service of neighbor, especially the poorest. (SRS 46)

7

Church and Society

A. Universality of Mission

CHRIST IS THE LIGHT of all nations. By her relationship with Christ, the Church is a kind of sacrament or sign of intimate union with God and of the unity of all mankind. She is also an instrument for the achievement of such union and unity. For this reason, following in the path laid out by its predecessors, this council wishes to set forth more precisely to the faithful and to the entire world the nature and encompassing mission of the Church. The conditions of this age lend special urgency to the Church's task of bringing all men to full union with Christ, since mankind today is joined more closely than ever before by social, technical, and cultural bonds. (LG 1)

All men are called to belong to the new People of God. Wherefore this people, while remaining one and unique, is to be spread throughout the whole world and must exist in all ages so that the purpose of God's will may be fulfilled. In the beginning, God made human nature one. After his children were scattered, he decreed that they should at length be united again. It was for this reason that God sent his son, whom he appointed heir of all things,

Church and Society

that he might be Teacher, King, and Priest of all, the Head of the new and universal people of the Sons of God. (LG 13)

It follows that among all the nations of the earth there is but one People of God, which takes its citizens from every race, making them citizens of a kingdom which is of a heavenly and not an earthly nature. Since the kingdom of Christ is not of this world, the Church or People of God takes nothing away from the temporal welfare of any people by establishing that kingdom. Rather does she foster and take to herself, insofar as they are good, the ability, resources, and customs of each people. Taking them to herself she purifies, strengthens, and ennobles them. (LG 13)

Drawn from the treasures of Christ's teaching, the proposals of this sacred synod look to the assistance of every man of our time, whether he believes in God or does not explicitly recognize him. Their purpose is to help men gain a sharper insight into their full dignity so that they can fashion the world more to man's surpassing dignity, search for a brotherhood which is universal and more deeply rooted, and meet the urgencies of our age with a gallant and unified effort born of love. (GS 91)

Undeniably this conciliar program is but a general one in several of its parts—and deliberately so, given the immense variety of situations and forms of human culture in the world. Indeed, while it presents teaching already accepted in the Church, the program will have to be further pursued and amplified, since it often deals with matters in a constant state of development. Still, we have relied on the Word of God and the Spirit of the Gospel. Hence we entertain the hope that many of our proposals will be able to bring substantial benefit to everyone, especially after they have been adapted to individual nations and mentalities by the faithful, under the guidance of their pastors. (GS 91)

By virtue of her mission to shed on the whole world the radiance of the Gospel message and to unify under one Spirit all men of whatever nation, race, or culture, the Church stands forth as a sign of the brotherliness which allows honest dialogue and invigorates it. (GS 92)

Such a mission requires in the first place that we foster within the Church herself mutual esteem, reverence, and harmony, through the full recognition of lawful diversity. Thus all those who compose the one People of God, both pastors and the general faithful, can engage in dialogue with ever-abounding fruitfulness. For the bonds which unite the faithful are mightier than anything which divides them. Hence, let there be unity in what is necessary, freedom in what is unsettled, and charity in any case. (GS 92)

Mindful of the Lord's saying: "By this all men will know that you are my disciples, if you have love one for one another" (John 13:35), Christians cannot yearn for anything more ardently than to serve the men of the modern world ever more generously and effectively. Therefore, holding faithfully to the Gospel and benefitting from its resources and united with every man who loves and practices justice, Christians have shouldered a gigantic task demanding fulfillment in this world. Concerning this task they must give a reckoning to him who will judge every man on the last day. (GS 53)

The church acknowledges the contributions made by other religions, Christian and non-Christian, and encourages collaboration with them.

The Catholic Church rejects nothing of what is true and holy in these religions. She has a high regard for the manner of life and conduct, the precepts and doctrine which, although differing in many ways from her own teaching, nonetheless, often reflect a ray of that truth which enlightens all men. Yet she proclaims and is duty bound to proclaim without fail, Christ who is the way, the truth, and the life (John 14:6). In him, in whom God reconciled all things to himself (2 Cor 5:18–19), men find the fullness of their religious life. (*Nostra Aetate,* NA 2)

The church, therefore, urges her sons to enter with prudence and charity into discussion and collaboration with members of other religions. Let Christians, while witnessing to their own faith and way of life acknowledge, preserve, and encourage the spiritual and moral truths found among non-Christians, also their social life and culture. (NA 2)

B. Church and Social Responsibility

During the last hundred years the Church has repeatedly expressed her thinking, while closely following the continuing development of the social question. She has certainly not done this in order to recover former privileges or to impose her own vision. Her sole purpose has been care and responsibility for man, who has been entrusted to her by Christ himself. (CA 53)

This, and this alone, is the principle which inspires the church's social doctrine. The Church has gradually developed that doctrine in a systematic way, above all in the century that has followed the date we are commemorating (1891 *Rerum Novarum*), precisely because the horizon of the Church's whole wealth of doctrine is man in his concrete reality as sinful and righteous. (CA 53)

Today, the Church's social doctrine focuses especially on man as he is involved in a complex network of relationships with modern societies. The human sciences and philosophy are helpful for interpreting man's central place within society and for enabling him to understand himself better as a "social being." However, man's true identity is only fully revealed to him through faith, and it is precisely from faith that the Church's social teaching begins. While drawing upon all of the contributions made by the sciences and philosophy, her social teaching is aimed at helping man on the path of salvation. (CA 54)

Christian anthropology therefore is really a chapter of theology and, for this reason, the Church's social doctrine, by its concern for man and by its interest in him and the way he conducts himself in the world, "belongs to the field . . . of theology and particularly moral theology" (SRS 41). The theological dimension is needed both for interpreting and solving present-day problems in human society. It is worth noting that this is true in contrast both to the "atheistic" solution, which deprives man of one of his basic dimensions, namely the spiritual one, and to permissive and consumerist solutions, which under various pretexts seek to convince man that he is free from every law and from God himself, thus imprisoning him within a selfishness which ultimately harms both him and others. (CA 55)

It is above all a question of interdependence, sensed as a system determining relationships in the contemporary world, in its economic, cultural, political, and religious elements, and accepted as a moral category. When interdependence becomes recognized in this way, the correlative response as a moral and social attitude, as a "virtue," is solidarity. This then is not a feeling of vague compassion or shallow distress at the misfortunes of so many people, both near and far. On the contrary, it is a firm and persevering determination to commit oneself to the common good, that is to say, to the good of all and of each individual, because we are all really responsible for all. This determination is based on the solid conviction that what is hindering full development is that desire for profit and that thirst for power already mentioned. These attitudes and "structures of sin" are only conquered—presuming the help of divine grace—by a diametrically opposed attitude, a commitment to the good of one's neighbor with the readiness, in the gospel sense, to "loose oneself" for the sake of the other instead of exploiting him for one's own advantage. (SRS 38)

C. Some Characteristics of Church Teaching

1. Mother and Teacher of Nations

The Catholic Church has been established by Jesus Christ as mother and Teacher of nations, so that all who in the course of centuries come to her loving embrace may find salvation as well as the fullness of a more excellent life. To this Church, "the pillar and mainstay of the truth" (1 Tim 3:15), her most holy Founder has entrusted the double task of begetting sons unto herself and of educating and governing those whom she begets, guiding with maternal providence the life both of individuals and of peoples. The lofty dignity of this life she has always held in the highest respect and guarded with watchful care. (MM 1)

2. Continuity and Renewal

The popes have not failed to throw fresh light by means of those messages upon new aspects of the social doctrine of the Church. As a result, this doctrine, beginning with the outstanding contribution of Leo XIII and enriched by the successive contributions of the magisterium, has now become an updated doctrinal "corpus." It builds up gradually, as the Church, in the fullness of the word revealed by Christ Jesus and with the assistance of the Holy Spirit, reads events as they unfold in the course of history. She thus seeks to lead people to respond, with the support of rational reflection and the human sciences, to their vocation as responsible builders of earthly society. (SRS 1)

3. Dynamic and Open to Options

Our purpose is to draw attention to a number of questions which because of their urgency, extent, and complexity must in the years to come take first place among the preoccupations of Christians, so that with other men the latter may dedicate themselves to solving the new difficulties which put the future of man in jeopardy. It is necessary to situate the problems created by the modern economy in the wider context of a new civilization. These problems include human conditions of production, fairness in the exchange of goods and in the division of wealth, the significance of the increased needs of consumption, and the sharing of responsibility. In the present changes, which are so profound and so rapid, each day man discovers himself anew, and he questions himself about the meaning of his own being and of his collective survival. Reluctant to gather the lessons of a past that he considers over and done with and too different from the present, man nevertheless needs to have light shed upon his future—a future which he perceives to be uncertain as it is changing—by permanent eternal truths. These are truths which are certainly greater than man but, if he so wills, he can himself find their traces. (OA 7)

In the face of so many new questions, the Church makes an effort to reflect in order to give an answer in its own sphere to men's expectations. If today the problems seem original in their breadth and their urgency, is man without the means of solving them? It is with all of its dynamism that the social teaching of the Church accompanies men in their search. If it does not intervene to authenticate a given structure or to prepare a ready-made model, it does not thereby limit itself to recalling general principles. It develops through reflection applied to the changing situations of this world, under the driving force of the Gospel as a source of renewal when its message is accepted in its totality and with all its demands. It also develops with the sensitivity proper to the Church which is characterized by a disinterested will to serve and by attention to the poorest. (OA 42)

In concrete situations, and taking account of solidarity in each person' s life, one must recognize a legitimate variety or possible options. The same Christian faith can lead to different commitments. The Church invites all Christians to take up a double task of inspiring and of innovating, in order to make structures evolve, so as to adapt them to the real needs of today. From Christians who at first sight seem to be in opposition, as a result of starting from different options, she asks an effort at mutual understanding of the other's positions and motives; loyal examination of one's own behavior and its correctness will suggest to each one an attitude of more profound charity which, while recognizing the differences, believes nonetheless in the possibility of convergency and unity. "The bonds which unite the faithful are mightier than anything which divides them" (GS 92). (OA 50)

4. Not Technical Solutions or Fixed Models

The Church does not have technical solutions to offer for the problems of underdevelopment as such. For the Church does not propose economic and political systems or programs, nor does she show preference for one or the other, provided that human dignity is properly respected and promoted, and provided she herself is allowed the room she needs to exercise her ministry in the world. (SRS 41)

But the Church is an "expert in humanity," which leads her necessarily to extend her religious mission to the various fields in which men and women expend their efforts in search of the always relative happiness which is possible in this world, in line with their dignity as persons. (SRS 41)

The Church has no models to present; models that are real and truly effective can only arise within the framework of different historical situations, through the effort of all those who responsibly confront concrete problems in all their social, economic, political, and cultural aspects as these interact with one another. For such a task the Church offers her social teaching as an indispensable and ideal orientation, a teaching which, as already mentioned, recognizes the positive value of the market and of enterprise but which at the same time points out that these need to be orientated toward the common good. (CA 43)

5. Option for the Poor

Here we indicate one of the characteristic themes and guidelines dealt with by the magisterium in recent years: the option or love of preference for the poor. This is an option, or a special kind of primacy in the exercise of Christian charity, to which the whole tradition of the Church bears witness. It affects the life of each Christian inasmuch as he or she seeks to imitate the life of Christ, but it applies equally to our social responsibilities and hence to our manner of living and to the logical decisions to be made concerning the ownership and use of goods. (SRS 42)

Today, furthermore, given the worldwide dimension which the social question has assumed, this love of preference for the poor, and the decisions which it inspires in us, cannot but embrace the immense multitude of the hungry, the needy, the homeless, those without medical care, and, above all, those without hope of a better future. It is impossible not to take account of the existence of these realities. To ignore them would be to become like the "rich man" who pretended not to know the beggar Lazarus lying at his gate (Luke 16:19–31). (SRS 42)

Bibliography

1971 Synod of Bishops. *Justice in the World.* No pages. http://www.shc.edu/theolibrary/resources/synodjw.htm.
Benedict XVI. *Caritas in Veritate.* No pages. http://www.vatican.va/holy_father/benedict_xvi/encyclicals/documents/hf_ben-xvi_enc_20090629_caritas-in-veritate_en.html.
———. *Deus Caritas Est.* No pages. http://www.vatican.va/holy_father/benedict_xvi/encyclicals/documents/hf_ben-xvi_enc_20051225_deus-caritas-est_en.html.
John XXIII. *Mater et Magistra.* No pages. http://www.vatican.va/holy_father/john_xxiii/encyclicals/documents/hf_j-xxiii_enc_15051961_mater_en.html.
———. *Pacem in Terris.* No pages. http://www.vatican.va/holy_father/john_xxiii/encyclicals/documents/hf_j-xxiii_enc_11041963_pacem_en.html.
John Paul II. *Centesimus Annus.* No pages. http://www.vatican.va/holy_father/john_paul_ii/encyclicals/documents/hf_jp-ii_enc_01051991_centesimus-annus_en.html.
———. *Dives in Misericordia.* No pages. http://www.vatican.va/holy_father/john_paul_ii/encyclicals/documents/hf_jp-ii_enc_30111980_dives-in-misericordia_en.html.
———. *Laborem Exercens.* No pages. http://www.vatican.va/holy_father/john_paul_ii/encyclicals/documents/hf_jp-ii_enc_14091981_laborem-exercens_en.html.
———. "Letter to Families from Pope John Paul II *Gratissimam Sane.*" No pages. http://www.vatican.va/holy_father/john_paul_ii/letters/1994/documents/hf_jp-ii_let_02021994_families_ en.html.

Bibliography

———. "Peace with God the Creator, Peace with All of Creation." No pages. http://www.vatican.va/holy_father/john_paul_ii/messages/peace/documents/hf_jp-ii_mes_19891208_xxiii-world-day-for-peace_en.html.

———. *Redemptor Hominis*. No pages. http://www.vatican.va/holy_father/john_paul_ii/encyclicals/documents/hf_jp-ii_enc_04031979_redemptor-hominis_en.html.

———. *Sollicitudo Rei Socialis*. No pages. http://www.vatican.va/holy_father/john_paul_ii/encyclicals/documents/hf_jp-ii_enc_30121987_sollicitudo-rei-socialis_en.html.

———. *Veritatis Splendor*. No pages. http://www.vatican.va/holy_father/john_paul_ii/encyclicals/documents/hf_jp-ii_enc_06081993_veritatis-splendor_en.html.

Leo XIII. *Rerum Novarum*. No pages. http://www.vatican.va/holy_father/leo_xiii/encyclicals/documents/hf_l-xiii_enc_15051891_rerum-novarum_en.html.

Paul VI. *Evangelii Nuntiandi*. No pages. http://www.vatican.va/holy_father/paul_vi/apost_exhortations/documents/hf_p-vi_exh_19751208_evangelii-nuntiandi_en.html.

———. *Octogesimo Adveniens*. No pages. http://www.vatican.va/holy_father/paul_vi/apost_letters/documents/hf_p-vi_apl_19710514_octogesima-adveniens_en.html.

———. *Populorum Progression*. No pages. http://www.vatican.va/holy_father/paul_vi/encyclicals/documents/hf_p-vi_enc_26031967_populorum_en.html.

———. "Visit to the United Nations. Speech to the United Nations Organization." No pages. http://www.va/holy_father/paul_vi/speeches/1965/documents/hf_p-vi_spe_19651004_united-nations_fr.html.

Pius XI. *Quadragismo Anno*. No pages. http://www.vatican.va/holy_father/pius_xi/encyclicals/documents/hf_p-xi_enc_19310515_quadragesimo-anno_en.html.

Pontifical Council for Justice and Peace. *Compendium of the Social Doctrine of the Church*. No pages. http://www.vatican.va/roman_curia/pontifical_councils/justpeace/documents/rc_pc_justpeace_doc_20060526_compendio-dott-soc_en.html.

———. *Towards Reforming the International Financial and Monetary System in the Context of Global Public Authority*. No pages. http://www.vatican.va/roman_curia/pontifical_councils/justpeace/documents/rc_pc_justpeace_doc_20111024_nota_en.html.

Second Vatican Council. *Dignitatis Humanae*. No pages. http://www.vatican.va/archive/hist_councils/ii_vatican_council/index.htm.

———. *Gaudem et Spes*. No pages. http://www.vatican.va/archive/hist_councils/ii_vatican_council/documents/vat-ii_const_19651207_gaudium-et-spes_en.html.

———. *Gravissimum Educationis*. No pages. http://www.vatican.va/archive/hist_councils/ii_vatican_council/documents/vat-ii_decl_19651028_gravissimum-educationis_en.html.

———. *Lumen Gentium*. No pages. http://www.vatican.va/archive/hist_councils/ii_vatican_council/documents/vat-ii_const_19641121_lumen-gentium_en.html.

———. *Nostra Aetate*. No pages. http://www.vatican.va/archive/hist_councils/ii_vatican_council/documents/vat-ii_decl_19651028_nostra-aetate_en.html.

Subject Index

authority, 19–21, 108, 116;
    civil, 46, 69, 71, 113;
    government, 74;
    political, 100–2;
    public, 77, 91, 100–102, 114;
    world, 82

capitalism, 67, 76–78, 89
charity, 52, 87, 125;
    in the Church, 2, 34, 120;
    and the economy, 70, 72, 87;
    and evangelization, 115;
    in marriage, 27;
    and politics, 105–6;
    in society, 17–8, 56;
    universal, 58
Christ, 8, 10, 11, 27, 41, 72, 90, 106, 125;
    and the Church, 116, 118–120, 121, 122–23;
    and human dignity, 2;
    and death 7;
    kingdom of, 52–53;
    and marriage, 27–28, 31;
    the message of, 48–49;
    redemption in, 87

common good,
    international, 119;
    universal, 8, 20–21, 44, 47, 65, 82, 93, 114
companionship, 6–7
community, 41–42, 87;
    and culture, 47–48;
    and the economy, 72, 74, 95;
    and education, 32–34;
    and emigration, 40;
    and disabled persons, 98;
    of the faithful, 48;
    family, 25;
    human, 37, 42, 78;
    international community, 23, 44, 80–82, 85, 112;
    political, 45–46, 71, 100–17;
    and unemployment, 99;
    world, 8, 15, 21, 22–23, 91
conflict,
    between labor and capital, 89-90;
    regional, 21, 24, 48, 56, 68, 83
conscience, 5, 7, 10-12, 31, 34–35, 38, 60, 61, 92, 106, 108–9
consumerism, 52, 83, 85

Subject Index

culture, 8, 9, 34, 40, 47–48, 48–49, 57, 61, 85, 88, 112, 119

death, 7, 22, 52, 92
destitution, 59
dignity, human, 1–24, 53, 54, 97–98, 101, 110, 124
disarmament, 109–10
divine law, 12, 31, 38
duty, 6;
    of the Church, 50, 69, 90, 115, 120;
    civic, 14, 52, 71, 73, 77, 82, 93, 99, 104;
    to God, 10, 11;
    of marriage, 30, 31;
    of nations, 58, 80;
    to other persons, 16;
    of parents, 27;
    to preserve life, 16;
    of work, 14, 94–95

ecology, 83–4;
    human, 31;
    social, 44
economy, 53, 76;
    and the Church, 124–25;
    and disarmament, 109–10;
    economic growth, 51, 55;
    economic rights, 14–15, 93;
    and the environment, 84;
    inequality in, 56, 91;
    justice in the, 68–75;
    international, 79–83;
    and labor, 86, 89–90, 95, 96–99;
    and ownership, 75–76, 76–77;
    and population, 36–37, 39–40;
    and society, 42–43, 57, 61–64, 77–78, 93–94, 100, 112–14, 122, 123;
    and theology, 65–66, 115–17;
    and urbanization, 43
education, 32–34, 44, 51, 55, 57, 62, 79, 92, 113;
    of children, 13; 26–27, 33, 98;
    and the Church, 33;
    civic and political, 105;
    ecological, 84–85;
    religious, 13, 27, 32, 34–35, 38;
    rights to, 9, 32;
    sexual, 33
emigration, 15, 40
employment, 43–44, 44, 51, 64, 72, 91, 95–96, 97
environment, 21, 31, 39, 44, 48, 51, 73, 83–85, 103
evangelization, 35, 68, 114, 114–5, 116

family, 13–14, 43, 47, 55;
    and Christ, 41;
    and the Church, 69;
    and education, 32, 85;
    and emigration, 15, 40;
    human, 15, 20, 21, 34, 47, 52, 70, 82, 83, 91, 107, 111;
    and marriage, 25–29, 29, 31;
    of nations, 44, 85;
    and population, 26;
    the right to, 13, 103
Food and Agriculture Organization (FAO), 59
freedom, 5–6, 10, 17, 17-18, 19, 33–34, 42, 53, 73, 77, 78;
    lack of, 31, 39;
    political, 51, 106;
    religious, viii, 11–13, 22, 104

globalization, viii, 19, 81–2, 90
government,
    choice of, 102–3;
    civil, 46;
    and the economy, 70, 74, 76;
    and globalization, 81;
    and population, 38–39;
    relations between, 113;
    and religion, 12; 81;
    and rights, 101–2;

Subject Index

and war, 109

Holy Spirit, 4, 10, 123

immigration, 15
intelligence, 4, 8, 48, 51, 53, 103
international cooperation, 37, 79
international debt, 63
international law, 20
international organizations, 55, 64, 80, 92, 94, 98
international relations, 94, 108–9, 115
international trade, 80

John XXIII, Pope, 7, 16, 19, 21, 59
John Paul II, Pope, 50, 60, 82, 86
justice, 10, 52–53, 106, 120;
    and common good, 46;
    economic, 67–68, 70–85;
    and education, 34–35;
    injustice, 10, 35, 54–6, 74, 83, 88, 105, 115;
    and labor, 96;
    and liberation theology, 114–15;
    and peace, 107–8, 110–11;
    right to, 15 23;
    social, vii, 58, 70;
    and society, 17–18;
    and work, 14, 94

labor, 86–99;
    and ownership, 75-76;
    and rights, 94–96;
    and society, 91–92
Latin American Episcopal Conference, 45
Leo XIII, Pope, 10, 46, 67, 68, 69, 86, 93, 102, 123
liberation theology, 114–17
love, 18;
    conjugal, 29-30, 30–31;
    divine, 27, 30;
    and marriage, 25, 26, 27, 28

marriage, 13;
    and the family, 25–32
mission, universality of, 49, 118–19, 125

ownership, 72–73, 125;
    private, 70, 73, 75–76, 76–77, 78, 95;
    public, 75–76, 77

Paul, Apostle, 17, 102
Paul VI, Pope, 21, 50, 60, 81
peace, 48, 63, 64, 94, 107–112, 113, 114, 115;
    and education, 32;
    world, 20, 35, 56, 83, 107–112
Pius XI, Pope, 42, 69, 74
Pius XII, Pope, 14, 15, 69, 110, 112
politics,
    and education, 84;
    and the Church, 105–7, 124–25;
    and community, 19–20, 20–21, 45–47, 71, 100–17;
    and freedom, 51;
    and leaders, 64, 99;
    and oppression, 62;
    and participation, 15, 57;
    and society, 17–18;
    and tyranny, 75;
    and socio-economics, 75, 76;
    world politics, 22, 59, 61, 65, 112–14
population, 26, 36–40, 43–44, 54–55, 61, 63, 64, 84
public affairs, 15, 103

rights, 7–15, 22, 52;
    to assemble, 14, 43, 93–94, 101;
    of the Church, 69;
    and duties, 16–17, 17–18;
    and the economy, 13–14, 70, 71, 74, 75;
    to education, 32, 103;
    to emigrate, 15, 40;
    of the family, 28–29, 103;

Subject Index

rights (cont.)
    of government officials, 38;
    of the individual, 55–56, 62;
    and labor, 40, 86, 91, 93–94, 94–95, 96, 103;
    and ownership, 76–77, 78;
    of political communities, 19–20;
    to political participation, 15, 100, 101, 104;
    and religious freedom, 104;
    universal human, 11, 16, 22–23, 23, 38, 55, 78, 93, 94, 98–99, 101, 103, 114, 117

socialism, 43, 67, 76, 77

Thomas Aquinas, Saint, 19

unemployment, 9, 62, 98

United Nations, 21, 22–23, 56
Universal Declaration of Human Rights, 22–23
urbanization, 43–44

wisdom, 4, 22;
    divine, 36
work,
    and capitalism, 78;
    and disabled persons, 98;
    and emigration, 39–40, 96–97;
    and man, 88–90;
    and organization, 92–94;
    purpose of, 87–88;
    the right to, 13–14;
    and rights of workers, 94–96;
    and society, 57, 61, 91–92;
    spirituality of, 90–91;
    and unemployment, 98–99

Source Index

Address of Paul VI to the General Assembly of the United Nations (PUN), 21–22, 35

Caritate in Veritate (CV), 2, 64
Catechism of the Catholic Church, 6
Centisimus Anus (CA), 38, 48, 68, 77–78, 85, 94, 97–98, 103–4, 105, 121–22, 125
Compendium of the Social Doctrine of the Church (CSDC), 53

Deus Caritas Est (DC), 90-91
Dignitatus Humanae (DH), 10–13
Dives in Miericordia (DM), 54

Ecological Crisis (EC), 83, 84-85
Evangelii Nuntiandi (EN), 114–117
Gaudium et Spes (GS), 1–6, 7, 25–28, 29, 30, 31, 37–39, 41, 44–45, 47–48, 49, 52–53, 70–73, 74, 76–77, 79, 86–87, 91, 93, 95–97, 100–2, 103, 104–5, 105–6, 107–9, 111–12, 119–20, 124
Gravissimum Educationis (GE), 32–34
Gratissimam Sane (GA), 6

Justice in the World (JW), 35, 74

Laborum Execrens (LE), 40, 78–79, 87–89, 90, 93, 94, 95, 98–99
Lumen Gentium (LG), 41, 118–19

Mater et Magistra (MM), 36–37, 41–43, 57, 69, 70, 74–75, 76, 91–92, 94–95, 112, 122

Nostra Aetate (NA), 120

Octogesimo Adveniens (OA), 43–44, 83, 92, 123–24

Pacem in Terris (PT), 7–10, 13–21, 22–23, 34–35, 39, 43, 45–47, 100, 1023, 107, 109–111, 113–14
Populorum Progressio (PP), 50–52, 54–56, 58–60, 73, 106–7

Quadragesimo Anno (QA), 74, 93, 98

Radio Message, Aug. 24, 1939, 111
Radio Message, June 1, 1941, 14
Radio Message, Dec. 24, 1941, 110
Radio Message, Dec. 24, 1944, 15
Redemptor Hominus (RH), 2, 87
Rerum Novarum (RN), 67, 68, 86, 92-93

Source Index

Sollicitudo Rei Socialis (SRS), 23–24, 39–40, 50, 60–64, 65–66, 80, 83-84, 104, 117, 122, 123, 124–25, 125

Toward Reforming the International Financial and Monetary Systems in the Context of Global Public Authority (TR Conclusions), 80–83

Veritatis Splendor (VS), 1–2, 6, 28, 30, 90

www.ingramcontent.com/pod-product-compliance
Lightning Source LLC
Chambersburg PA
CBHW070913160426
43193CB00011B/1440